Invisible Poets

Anthology 2

FUNDRAISING IN AID OF

Save the Children

WHEELSONG

BOOKS

First published by
Wheelsong Books
United Kingdom

© Invisible Poets, 2025

Print ISBN: 9-798-30967-222-6

Contents

Foreword

Invisible Poets Anthology 2 features more than 240 poems. This book is the result of a rigorous selection process. To be eligible for inclusion, each poem had to be performed on *Live Poets Society*. Regular viewers will know that only the best poetry features on the shows, which are broadcast live across the *Invisible Poets* Facebook network from the UK, the USA, Brazil and other countries. The shows' presenters are all very knowledgeable about poetry, but they also have diverse tastes. As a result, the poetry in this anthology is diverse, with a wide variety of themes, styles and formats. That means there should be something for everyone within these pages.

Invisible Poets Anthologies 2 and 3 commemorate the second anniversary of the *Invisible Poets* online group, which in two years, has gained more than 50,000 members.

Your purchase of the anthologies will not only benefit all the poets who are represented within these pages by gaining them a wider audience; it will also go a long way toward supporting children in crisis. Proceeds from the Amazon sales of this book will be donated to *Save the Children*—a worldwide relief fund that provides children in warzones and disaster areas with food, medicine, clothing, shelter—and eventually—education. It's a very worthy cause and we thank you for your valuable support.

Steve Wheeler
Poet and Founder
Invisible Poets and
Wheelsong Books

February, 2025

The Fear of Silence

Martin Gedge

Deep behind
These hollow eyes
Dark as pitch
And stitched with lies
To hang around
A feast of flies
That ties
This broken soul
For hurt
In chain
It shall remain
The mark of choice
A voice in flame
To burn with spit
With grit and grain
To stain
The pain I know
For fear
And hate
Beyond this gate
I'm sure that those
Can all relate
For what you see
Or tolerate
Debate my state as well
For silent still
This evil mill
To push the pin
And pop the pill
There is no time
To find and fill
The thrill or will to tell
For of thy skin
What harbours in
From flesh and bone
Of stone and gin
Prepare to take it

On the chin
To spin this grin I hide
Through lock and key
I fancy thee
Not what you bought
Or thought of me
But true to form
And born to be
This storm to brew inside…

Reminisce and Renew

Terry Bridges

Memories drip into pools of dreams.
A recreated past where love is kind.
So much torment and heartache we suffer,
Then focus. Seek and you will find.

A quiet place for passion re-assessed,
Unravelling the thread of our lives.
Braving the labyrinthine obstacles,
Fate scissors us through with knives.

The scales of justice gravitate to one side.
No one is ever perfectly in balance.
Typhoons sail through us like the wind,
But purity shields us from malice.

Safe harbour, docking where we started from,
Eternal recurrence. The dawn emerges.
A smudge of light on a far horizon,
Painting with colour the dark's edges.

What new delight awaits its birth.
The brilliant sun slowly arises.
Fortune favours every adventure,
The promised morning pregnant with surprises.

Belleza Maldita

Gregory Richard Barden

dark, deep ...

warm-black arms of
an endless night wrap me ...
my head thrown back in abdication
arms spread wide in surrender
falling backward ...
back, back ... onto a hard dogwood blackness
nails of my own stark weakness
fasten my hands to a weighty tree of
terrifying introspection ...
a poison saturates my blood—
courses with its curses through the very
vessel my soul inhabits—
dictates to me by the minutes the movements
of my muscles ...
the states of my organs—
responses and emotions, actual
like the visceral, mighty hand of some
morbidly jealous god
squeezing the true and the good from every
last cell of my being—
the strength and health built by a lifetime
of good habit and task
torn asunder by a guileful beast
a duplicitous, faceless monster that I invited in
from wintertide like some
pitiful, starving fawn ...
oh, it IS pitiful in its treachery
and it starves ... oh yes, it starves
with a hunger for souls and
lives and accomplishments and truth
it eats them all with a lust unending and
a ravenous fury
laughing at you with a Cheshire grin
your crimson blood on its shining, chiselled teeth
and while you tremble in horror at its stark visage

19

while you stare transfixed into
the lifeless black eyes,
the face changes ...
the abomination transforms into a
beauty so pure and compelling
that your only thought and desire and compulsion
is to drink it in with a kiss as deep
as the Universe itself ...
to pour yourself into it with every
passion and emotion you can scrape from the
ice-flaked walls of your conscience
to merge with it—
to join with it in all abandon and care
and give yourself, whole
to the dim, shadowy vehemence complete
while the deafening roar of
your own screams and scratchings
plays a somber requiem, final
a sickly sweet song ...
of obliteration.

Glistening in the Golden Haze

Donna Smith

Under the bright azure blue sky
We sat taking in the sun's rays,
As they cast a warm yellow hue,
Glistening in the golden haze.

The birds and bees' flit and fly by
Between the flowers as I gaze,
Their colours radiant and true,
Glistening in the golden haze.

A wondrous sight cast on the eye,
How I wish I could spend my days
Watching the earth bloom and renew,
Glistening in the golden haze.

On the Silvermines Mountain

Joe Callanan

Downwind away from him in the trees
I saw his breathing bellow white
Then it was carried off on a jagged breeze
I saw ragged antlers told a recent fight

It was winter time of year
When I followed that big red deer
I could smell he was near
His soft scent filled the freezing air

The cold was cutting me in two
Though I dared not move one little bit
My balance corrected an inch or two
He leapt high as if he'd been hit

I had followed him twice before
Once back up toward the little caves
Through forests again onto our lakeshore
Down from the Highland mythic graves

Soon he'd walk on barley oats or wheat
Winter sown along with my wish to meet
Beside an Oak standing with a noble deer
Our family shield out in cold open air

A distance I'll never reach much less pass
I see him bounding steadily away uphill
I'll head back now in time for evening mass
To say a prayer then thank God for the thrill

breathing in you...
Lana Martin

I breathe out songs
breathing you in...
this heart belongs...
in the air filled with musical keys
unlocking beginning of all my melodies
this heart composes and devotes...
to you
synchronous duets
random roulettes
spinning around prairies
stuck in my memories
of highlands
of mountains...
fresh breath of prelude to the end
introspection of life
that they apprehend
bend
and...
until the end
I'll breathe you in
I'll breathe out melodies
made of wild musk
made of colors denied
made in songs of dusk
until we collide...
Until we breathe out
In the twilight zone.

Yes, Let's

Ryan Morgan

Let's raise a glass
To being astonished
And drink in the surprise
Of every extra sip of life.

Let's toast to the truth,
That we are a portion
Of the bubbling wonder
That effervesces around us.

Let's trade our tales
Around company's warmth,
Feed the shared flame
We each carry within.

Let's sing to the stars
The song of our sun,
And proclaim to the night
The delight of our light.

Let's plunge our palms
Plumb into passion's pigments,
And press our enthusiasm
Onto the wall for all to see.

Let's dance unfettered
From fears of looking the fool,
And kick our candid heels through
Drifts of guileless glee.

And then, let's sleep
Like we are children.
Bathe, deep in our dream
And awaken renewed.

In all she is...

Carter George Rob

How I wish that I could show you
What my blue eyes have seen
That stir up all my emotions
And my senses while I dream

Such a wonderful experience
To live through night and day
Immense pleasure it gives me
That never ever fades away

I see sunrise, I see flowers
I see moonlight, I see stars
I see a kaleidoscope of colours
That brighten up my heart

I see radiant, I see lovely
I see exquisite, I see sublime
I see drop dead gorgeous
Through these eyes of mine

How I wish that I could show you
There's so much more than this
I love the way it makes me feel
There's beauty in all she is....

deep fakes of artificial aborigines
Matt Elmore

we identify your tribe

dopamine drips on obsessed like addicts
fuelled by endorphins endorsed by fanatics
possessed defined ply bland semantics
autocratic schemes in automatic mechanics

we see through your lies

slipped insidious in sips of ticking love hits
fixed on a fix for tips on getting more clicks
emulations of images suggest what fits
spinached split sandwiches, dark yet well-lit

we identify your disguise

gooped into groups of follow me please
feeding artificial sleaze on cold plastic knees
as screens teem preprogrammed blank sheen
to facilitate facilities inhuman and pristine

we withhold your prize
for designs refine to emulate human response
voiced images blink bunk flowing in fake fonts
like max headroom groomed in tombs haunt
synthetic thoughts caught wrongly ensconced

we detect your demise
projecting suggestions of empathetic traces
facsimile of smiles to pixilate faceless faces
devoid of determination or divine graces
a spammer scams scum in potted meat cases

we are human and wise
programmed to debase portions on plates
dished to fool innocents hungry for haste
oblivious to insidious cheats on the take
unoriginal aborigines passing off deep fakes
we can turn off your rise

Space Cowgirl Soliloquy

Linda Adelia Powers

Because there is a law such as gravity
the Universe can and will create itself
out of nothing.
—Stephen Hawking

Where did that law come from?
Gravity exists without matter and energy?
Where was our bubbly bouncy universe before?
Oh, it's a finite, expanding sphere like a balloon.
That can't be (you didn't answer the question)
The outside must be inside, it's a uni-verse.
There is no outside, it's everywhere.
Everywhere? Then how can it be at all limited?
Is there an infinity of space?

Infinity is just a concept, it doesn't correspond.
No, infinity is an endless number of numbers.
No, an infinity's not a number, it's the set of all
numbers produced by a function
A mathematical functional
A hologram of itself.
Well, there's a finite amount of matter/energy:
mattergy.

Therefore space is finite.
No, space goes on forever, you cannot escape.
Time is timeless, just a construct, a tool of
measurement.
Silly, the arrow of time obviously points forward.

Why so intrigued by all these insides and outs,
When Leibniz asks us to prove answers to:
"Will we ever know why anything exists,
Why is there something rather than nothing?"

Carved

Simone Ingle

Worlds apart,
but souls entwined.
Distance is insignificant,
you are always nearby.
Alluring creature,
how I love to amble along through your mind.
Stay slow, take my time.
You're the only one that invited me to dive in heart first,
without even meaning to,
take a step inside to see what I can find,
or to be more accurate what I couldn't uncover.
I sit and ponder,
wonder are there really any rocks I have left unturned,
after all this time do I really still know you?
The inner workings,
what makes you tick, tock, tick?
I can see from your smile,
parted lips,
the glimmer in your eyes,
the way you look at me seeing straight through mine,
going deeper in to the core.
How is it possible to see me the way you do?
Know more about me than I ever did,
see the real woman behind the mask,
understand from day one the being I would become?
You saw me at my worst.
Helped the dark tales and pain melt away,
made the demons disintegrate back to dust,
forcing them out from the shadows,
banishing them for good,
causing them to rot from the inside out
in a way of the purest beauty.
Your mind enticed me,
challenged me on all levels,
it still does to this day,
you are never far...
No matter how hard I would try,

you would always come back.
You are the only one that will always last,
unlike the rest you will never go off,
turn sour,
grow mould,
you're here for the long hall,
purely organic.
Free from GMOs you're perfect as you are,
the finest produce.
A beautiful soul.
Fallen fruit from mother nature's sweetest tree.
You make my inner self gasp each time we contact,
through eyes,
smiles,
touch,
collided minds,
wondrous thoughts in our own little universe.
A perfectly carved soul to me....

Galactic Noises
Martin Attard

The galaxy broadcasts to me
Constantly at low frequency
A static my subconscious hears
Through my bones not just my ears.
Analysed it is gibberish
No tonal changes deep and rich
We've searched for its hidden code
But none's been found so I am told.
But when I can find a quiet place
Far from the noisy human race
I let my brain absorb the transmission
So my stardust cells get their nutrition.

Take this Dust, Create a Star

Patrick Darnell

My wise friend there is much work to be done
A'fore seven deadly sins every setting sun,
If ever I am to gain paradise,
I hasten judgment in its pan-disguise.

Take a pill, sit very still, ambulate to wait,
A pill, a crutch, a stool, still inadequate.
Seven virtues, seven cords, I might have had,
Except for short stint as a deadbeat dad.

And greedy looking for shill outsourcing,
And cuckold at a very young courting,
Do not forget corporate silent quitter,
And a dubious loquacious gibber.

I was styled as rapacious in the womb
Apt to be an uptown, bright-headed bloom,
Hardwired rudiments in my character,
Unused in my socio-economic craters.

And now, how to take this dust of my life
To present my woebegone after-life?
Certainly only one proton remains
Useful to celestial starlight re-claims.

If I should outrun seven deadly sins
On this one day when I begin again,
As cleanly released from fecund flesh,
Could I be free too of infernal mesh?

Older now, am I also the wiser?
I've taken you on as my advisor

On Desire
E.C. McCaffrey

If I was dead and dead, I'll surely be.
When youth has fled, into infinity.
Would I recall the truth of hope's embrace?
Where in my dreams, I saw love face to face?
As faithful as the sun should rise each day.
Some ancient vow, that truth could find a way.
Where blood runs chaste and joins a common hope
And peace redeems the twine of heaven's rope.
Life's wealth could not be found in glittered gold.
But only when divinity is known.
That is the art of learning to believe.
For what is love? If not what we conceive
No greater worth, a soul could never find.
Than that of love that calls itself divine
And when I die, please hold this prayer for me.
That I would find the truth divinity.

In death's sweet hour my heart has one desire—
To quench the soul that begs for holy fire.

Shadow's Tale
Cliff Hancock

Standing at the crossroads of tomorrow's yesterday,
I took stock of every flip and flop I took along my way.

How I laughed at the circled path, decades deep with folly,
Where before the path I tore, deliberate with higher calling.

Had I never strayed along my way, perhaps I'd have a home.
Perhaps I'd have a wife and life somewhere beyond alone.

What did I learn on the trail I churned, waste deep within the mire?
That no dream I've seen makes me the king of my most base desire.

Embrace the Swan's Life
Kateleen Miado

Graceful, confident
Smoothly gliding on water
Neck arched, poised to strike
Alluring and tough
Quick to anger, do not try
Best to stay away

Admire her pure strength
Judge her brutality, as
She protects her own
Silvery feathers
Glistening in the moonlight
Still, yet powerful

Love and loyalty
Wings lift off towards the sky
Ready to take flight
Regal and divine
Transformed into so much more
Embrace the swan's life

Three Dead Pigeons
Trude Foster

Three dead pigeons came to mourn
they hung around from dusk till dawn
and knowing I was gravely ill
stayed perched upon my window-sill
then when it looked like I might stay
they clicked their beaks and flew away

Id Ink

Ryan Morgan

Far below my surface
Melodic fragments shift.
Formless as shadows
They coalesce like mist
On the mired moor of morning,
An expiration of inspiration.
Clouds within me forming
Anticipation of precipitation.

Are they krakens of the deep?
Leviathans of the Id?
They roam when I'm asleep,
Subconscious giant squid.
Their fins occasionally cut the surface
And they breach with playfulness,
Emerging from my abstract abyss,
Coasting the shallows of wakefulness.

With my tangled skein psyche
Should I lure them into my nets?
Or would they just capsize me
And drag me with them to the depths?
If I attempt to catch my dreams
Will my hand grasp at nothing?
A grail, a windmill, a mirage, or moonbeams
Like a pearl on the seafloor shimmering?
Its iridescence unattainable,
Refracting elusively,
Taunting like a rainbow:
A delusively illusive spectrality.

Or does inspiration lurk in the wrecks
Of what I've sunk in my life,
Feeding in the doleful depths
As psychological parasites?

Am I an Ahab or a Fisher King?

Though of course both bear the wounds
Inflicted by the very thing
They tried obsessively to harpoon.

Call Me Uriel

Gavin Prinsloo

The earth shakes and the ground quakes,
as my feet beguile the earth,
Consumed in fire I will never tire,
before Eden was my birth

I am the Light yet guard your sight,
for my fury burns with zeal,
From ages past my fury lasts,
imposing Heavens seal

I smite and have burned, to crimson turned,
laying waste to the tribes of man below,
I am a dream and an eternal scream,
as Ezra will surely know

Your soul is numb with things to come,
for prophecy destroys the mind,
I make the thunder speak and corpses reek,
for prophets are mine to find

Yet within my truth a probable cause to open doors,
For my wisdom lays my sword aside,
For mercy also guides my hand,
So seek and you shall find

In truth I raise my hand to understand,
and I know of things to come,
When the time is due, to my nature true,
I will undo what man has done

Red Tulips
Sheila Ann

My love is as deep as dying
Mounting on a winged horse
I came down flying with the wind,
Even the moon seen daily is untrue
And the eyes search for the stars
shimmering in the Orion blue,
Dreams of my heart gives me no pleasure
Garden of red tulips, withered
and the tiny grass was adamant,
Return back my stolen thought
My heart is in a frantic fosse,
As darkness say the dawn shall not come again
My silence fades into shadows,
I wander around like a lonely traveller in bane
Lost in the jungle of love, thorn in wane.

Door A-Crack
Karin J. Hobson

Synced as joined, no clown nor sun
Doorstep opens solely for one;
Audio strategically placed to hear
Beating in pellucid right ear;
What harkened at nite, arose light;
Chimed in with no gust of winds
Told the tale of sin and man;
Displaced was he too quickly to see
Greed was taken as better feed;
From heart to head ludicrous fed
Love for loving hearts sat dead;
Heart of man can slam door shut
as fast as he can without rebut;
Faith shall prove door a-crack;
Foot jam prevents rams to stack.

Sane

Terry Bridges

I own the silence
The night assembles
Riches galore in
Perpetual quiet
A forest of thought
Brooding memories
Come haphazardly
Into their presence
Planetary wars
Forgotten like dust
An echo of light
Splitting the ether
Telegrams transmit
Written paperless
Words proliferate
The essence of this
Multiplying black
Dousing midnight's flame
Cracks in the ceiling
Leaking brilliance
Dripping through evening
Fantasies remain
Occupy the space
In our tiny brain
Nothing like nothing
To investigate
Beyond galaxies
Universal pain
A touch of madness
Glimpses of reason
Lost and found again

Harbinger of Spring
Magda Giurea

Spring appeared in my way
With the white dress
of fragrant apple blossoms
Nature is sighing by the lake
Of my childhood
For the sake of the painting
Of our architect sun.

A few snowdrops petals
Fall into my small palms
And I feel the unmistakable aroma
Of March days like a newborn.

Hush
Emile Pinet

Artillery shells explode outside my door,
Hush, get on the floor.

Soldiers are murdering people on my street,
Hush, till they retreat.

Traumatized children are forbidden to cry,
Hush, or we'll all die.

Russia turned Ukraine into a killing zone,
Hush, we're not alone.

Artillery shells explode outside my door
as they've done before,
Hush, we are at war.

The Keeper of Missing Things

Lorna McLaren

He was the keeper of missing things,
I read it in the book,
all catalogued and dated
so he'd know just where to look.
He'd find all sorts on his travels
as he'd walk around the town
then advertise the missing things
so the owners would be found.
But many things just lay unclaimed
and with them he couldn't part
knowing they once belonged to someone
and just didn't have the heart.
From pretty buttons from a coat or dress
someone would proudly wear
to bobbles and silky ribbons
that fell from some child's hair.
Rings and bracelets and a locket too
were amongst the things he found,
why no-one came to claim them
it always did astound.
He wondered at these missing things
and what stories lay behind,
how they were parted from their owners
that were left for him to find.
Years rolled on, the collection grew
kept safely in his keep
still waiting there to be claimed
shelf upon shelf so deep.
Feeling his time was coming to an end
a letter he must leave,
with instructions on these missing things,
for someone to retrieve.
Simply asking his work be carried on,
to know the happiness it brings,
reuniting people with their treasures and to become
the new keeper of missing things.

I found his letter and his precious horde
so his work continues on
but hope that some other will take over
when my time has come and gone.
I'll leave a letter, just the way he did,
about all the pleasure that it brings
on seeing the smiles upon those faces
when reunited with treasured things.
I'll tell the story of the original keeper
to be sure he doesn't go unsung
for it's a never ending work in hand
and will be for years to come.
I must leave the story here for now
to catalogue and date these things
that add to the growing collection I have found
now I'm the keeper of missing things.

Inward Light
Rafik Romdhani

No path to take you to ample imagination
and no invisible wings
to wear upon shoulders born from mountains
and the serene appearance of a blue ocean.
No preset track for budding carnation
before it ascends like a flown lava
pushed upward by unknown momentum.
No butterfly knew it would bear
the colour of oranges and the eyes
of a wandering panda on both sides.
No poetry would levitate and dance
like a mural without the fuel of angst.
Words fly at the speed of an albatross
to pollinate the space with their powers.
No meaning to life except a heart
glowing red with millions of cinders
and no poetry without the inward light.

Pololu with Neena

Rufus Daigle

We carried stones to Pololu
You tasted my tears
The soap of the waves
Against short sighted barriers
The waterfall like the
Clarity in a necklace
Your kisses softer than
The snowflake rains
Sheets of implied pearls
Amulets jutting out from
God's masterpiece
Steps down to lau'hala buds
And changing footprints
Of open time
The valley like a Princess curled up in
A quilt of ancient flowers
Her sensual river paying homage to
the ocean with Kia logs
Sculptured in the lanai of the
Moors' sand
Your eyes like hands
of a puppeteer
The sun creates a window
Of your beauty
The Princess climaxing near our
wind laden sheets
Your hands illuminated
from a royal promise
I recycled your kisses into
Buddha's chosen
I left your tears that emerged as
diamonds with pololus' gift
Waves running towards us like the
retreads of our lives
Like water wheels in a
Sorcerers glass
You pulled my faucet of pain into your

Bosom song tide
Next to your Crown
Near your saffron
Glittered metaphors of how you
trained time
I love you more
I felt heaven laden men
Pigeons I their tongues
Slothfully crawling down the path
Of the erotic trail
Editing the breathe of masks leaving
the womb of Pololu
The fauna of your mother's spirit
next to my ear
Your opulent soul
Awakening a sorcerers' guilt
Your mothers' praise lay beside us
On matted hemp
Near a rainbows' lisp
Of gravity's song
Noted beauty
With soft candles
In your eyes
And lips the flavor of lilliquoi syrup
Fingers pulling tokens from
A monks poetic carcass

Burn

Terry Bridges

The quiet yells at the nothingness of night
A crackling pristine moon burns in pure heaven
Time to appreciate the astonishment of sight
Ice frosts the sashed window crisp and even

My happy solitude evaporates into thin air
These distant vistas beyond all comprehension
Can't you see exploding starlight everywhere?
This glorious life...this sweet release of tension

Peace encourages peace and deep darkness matters
Shade and light twin doppelganger shadows
We stand erect in silence mad as hatters
Amazed...drinking in the forests and meadows

This pale blue dot in a universe...cold...remote
Burn your existence to ashes...burn your boat

Winter Fingers

Trude Foster

Winter fingers
cool on my neck
sharp on my face
slaps the season into place

Winter fingers
jagged nails
frosty hair
claws my throat with icy air

Winter fingers
sharpened splinters
frigid stones
a punch with frozen knuckle bones

Primavera
Corey Reynolds

winter grass desirous of its green
waiting to be adored once again
never wanting to feel the sting
and the icy cover of winters chill
wishing for the friendship of flowers
and the return of the sun and its brilliance
waiting on the spring and its color
and longing for its wild wild hope

The Secret of Windchime Wood
Becky Topham

Let us walk, you and I
Whilst the sunshine is still in your eyes
The autumn in your glossy hair
And your flame haired canine by your side

By the looking glass lake
Past a heart at the neck of two swans
Left at the great fallen oak
Where the woodland is alive with song

And the whispering stream spills secrets
(Perhaps of those who came before)
Though it welcomes our tread amicably
And the foliage forms an intricate door

There we'll find the place
Where we often we spent our hours
As little girls—with spirits high—
Beneath trees as tall as towers

And shall we kindle a fire again
As we were often apt to do?

(Here, where the shadows are dark and long
And I only see the silhouette of you).

Shall it be as though you never died
When I spark a flame upon the wood?
Shall it cast a golden hue upon your skin
As nothing else earthly could?

And will you share your stories
Captivating my thought;
So I shall forget the sorrow—
Which the past three years have wrought?

Here you shall laugh, my twin
And it will echo through the trees
Amidst the squawk and song of birds
And the drunken hum of bees

And I shall remember my love for you
Before I admit I am here all alone
Surrounded by the fire's ashes
And trees trunks of milky bone

The birds grey and voiceless
The bees no longer abuzz
Flowers which forgot to bloom
And it becomes a forlorn looking wood

I pass the solitary swan
And she looks remorseful into my eye
We two -now alone in this world—
Beneath the darkening autumn skies

When you left—you stole the music,
The warmth, the laughter, the song
You were the secret of Windchime Wood
Where—together—we learnt to belong

Midnight Moon

J. T. Caine

I wrote a letter to the midnight moon
I told her hush and that
I'd be there soon
But
I'll be the first to say I don't know how
All my promises
Are empty now
And
I whispered love into this crowded room
Poured my soul into
A white-washed tomb
I
Don't want to live like I am broke in two
Can't see it from another
Point of view
She
Wants to know that I have found my place
I'm too afraid
I'll just be lost in space
When
I hear her calling, I can't see her face
I'm out of time and
Always out of place
My
Heart was open when she walked right out
Her view is better now
I have no doubt
Though
I can't help it if I hurt this way
It was her time to go
She couldn't stay
Now
I'll send my messages in rain so sweet
Walk the city streets
On worn out feet
Til
She comes around again, her sidelong smile

Waiting in the dark
I'll stay a while

Phillip Larkin Changes his Mind
Chris Brew

Librarian of the English word
I may well be, yet now refine
My marmoreal Valentine:
Change the notion, keep the beat.
Yes, that faint hint of the absurd
Is language I will not repeat.

If my mind is post-baroque
My soul's from ages, never still,
So I repent and take my fill,
Acknowledge that what's old is new.
I shall stand upon that Rock
The Gift I now can see as true.

The fools in coats and silly hats
Are not the essence, just the sign.
Through them still your Light can shine
And what they know I now must learn.
And though I find them mostly bats
They have fixed my atheistic turn.

The sharp and tender shock of Love,
The tender gauntlet, softened hand,
Reflects in us a tender band
That locks us to a better realm,
That keys us to a world above.
The Christian God is at the helm.

Selfish
Robert Speights

Trees don't bear fruit for themselves
Or breathe the air that they make
Won't eat the nuts on the ground
That fall when given a shake

Rivers don't drink their own water
Nor squeeze into bottles for self
Never bathing in their own streams
Or splash to refresh themself

The sun doesn't shine cause its dark
Doesn't rise to start its own days
It doesn't burn because it gets cold
Never enjoys its own rays

Clouds don't make rain cause they're thirsty
Don't make shade because they get hot
Move across skies to prevent boredom
Don't give themselves one single thought

Maybe I'm being ridiculous
Using a poem to simply discuss
The way we tend to be selfish
Thinking our life is all about us

Here Comes the Sun
Peter Rimmer

The stars shine a light at night
Our star steals the day
Sunlight daylight starlight
Blue light defines the sky
White light rainbow hued
A new day star-blessed
Here comes the sun.

Terlingua

Joan Eddie

At the Brewster County line
Where the desert
Meets the sky
The scorpion crawls and
The snake slithers
Under rocks to escape
The blazing sphere
Always there.

Terlingua's cracked
Scabbed earth
Draws lonely
Isolated souls
Haunted by past pain felt
Hidden in rusted
Airstream trailers
Or mud brick shelters built
Their naked doors
Weathered
By swirling storms of grit

This is a place God
Put aside
A place forgotten by all
But a few
A struggling raw place
Angry scrubland
Where dirt flourishes
A place of human
Tumbleweeds
Overlooked and
Seeking solace

Digesting Cherubs

J. Henry DeKnight

Feed me angels in the moonlight
I get hungry when I sleep
Hit me in the face with attitude
If my thoughts get way too deep
I'm all snug here in my bed
but it's nearly 2 am
Feed me angels as I wake up
I'm keep dreaming of all of them
Whisper quiet while I devour
Angel wings and angel power
Need angelic magic quick
In my bloodstream that is sick
Cross my heart but I won't die
Just a snack that loves to fly
Feed me angels in the moonlight
And don't ever ask me why ...

Bloody Song

Imelda Zapata Garcia

In the throes of ravenous, clutches grip
his tender heart, it rips, it drips
It holds his whole, entire song,
the one he wrote, where he belongs
This kindred soul, who's love is bound
entrapped in rapture of its sounds
Within loud treble, wrought with pain
in crowded clamor, it sustains
An ebbing cry, his rhyme endowed
forgotten dreams, time now allows
In this hymn, a rapturous reap
his tortured heaven, it seeps, it weeps

Blister

Tim Queen

sometimes
you have to lean into death
she says
because they've closed
the highland theater
for good
and birds chirp a strange cadence
no one smiles
behind the masks
and her soul
is an undefended country.

the sky is a broken umbrella
she sits beneath
in autumn skin
and the rain falls in
staccato...stiletto.

old woman
take my covid hand
we'll dance a broken waltz
down stumble streets.

beneath gasoline rainbows
we'll lean into death.
for tomorrow
is an empty house
and dreams arrive
as checks
on the 1st of the month
and the moon
is a dead fish belly.

Glittering Future

Ryan Morgan

It's raining silver
In that town over the foam,
A lustrous shimmer
That crowns each home.
Cleansing with its luminosity,
Washing away the sediment
Deposited by the storm's fury
And refreshing my sentiment.

Ahead there is light.
Prospects are not riddled with gloom.
Just look at the bright,
Coruscating, sprinkled bloom
On the slates that were surly and grey
Now adorned with beams
Just a short journey away:
Tomorrow's horizon gleams.

The Summit

Archie Papa

And just as the tears of joy did fall
so did the empire of youthful dreams
from nothing tallied the value of time
until priceless or so it seems

And so the heart would shallow time
and bear each stepping stone
on the path which love creates
we are never all alone

Moments will capture these memories
and fill in the voids of the past
taller the mountain of time will grow
the farther our shadows cast

Turquoise Memories

Rufus Daigle

Turquoise memories as rocks melt
And sand dials start at our feet
The ocean knows how love
Begins
Your chair is empty
But I remember your eyes
Like fallen diamonds
As I reach
The needle stops the quilt waits
Still I see the pater of your feet
The twist of your waist
The turn of your head
As your lovely face
Chokes my tears
How you run to me
And I care for all that you offer
Your words like silver to my tongue
Your tears like magnets to
My soul
You came when no one else cared
That day near the coat of the lamb
The sun like a blade
Your lips tying mine heart in knots
How could I forget

sonnets of secrets #5
(celestial infinite divinity)
Matt Elmore

minutes burn like meteors streak in skies
hours like comets circling in taunts
just as planetary bodies collide
we reconcile lies for truth and needs for wants

we exist as a nucleus of orbits
of souls swimming under wrinkles of flesh
unrolling cosmic scrolls painting portraits
of risen spirits buried in sunsets

reconciling light for dark shades of years
amongst chaos achieve lost serenity
beyond this casket our future frontiers
celestial infinite divinity

for all mundane moments ignorance does space
differences in action make to replace

Sunset Poet
Peter Rivers

Upon these dusty streets I write
Deep in thought, this pen I swirled
I scatter verse to fading light
Upon these dusty streets I write
This story like the day, ends in night
A view of shadows, that chase the world
Upon these dusty streets I write
Deep in thought, this pen I swirled

Reflections

Valerie Dohren

Behold the pregnant silvered moon
Full mirrored in the shimmering sea
And shining low at early dawn
The sun, as golden filigree

Reflecting in the dancing waves
To crown each glorious day anew
The sky a burning oriflamme
Soft glist'ning in the morning dew

And see above the drifting clouds
As o'er the land their shadows creep
Like ghostly spectres ling'ring on
The hills and valleys, nestling deep

Then hear the mighty oceans break
Against the rocks, so cold and grey,
Resounding 'cross the des'late shores
To crash, untamed, then fade away

And as above then so below
The large reflected in the small
So too the all-pervading power
Lies deep in every living soul

Reflected in each beating heart
Each single atom, small yet vast,
And there within each grain of sand
The boundless universe is cast

And so the threads of thought unwind
Each fantasy, inspired to spin
Reflections of the inner self
Where all is still, so still within

Without Pain

Graeme Stokes

If the mighty rivers flowed no pain,
There could be no source of joy
If in an open heart it never rains,
Then its beats could not rejoice
Without the sacrifice of selfless tears,
There could be no gift of laughter
And if the journey held no woes or fears,
There'd be no thrills of what comes after
Without the learning curve of loss,
A path of gain cannot be found
A rolling stone shall see no moss,
If it shifts in delinquent clouds
Devoid of the weight of heavy frowns,
Unburdened smiles would surely drop
And to turn sorrow upside down,
Pure faith must stay on top
Without a sense of intrepid adventure,
There's no story to be told
Without the probing of every dimension,
There's no planting of new bulbs
If procrastination stays rock still,
A deja vu state of tedium
The ifs fade in ailing appeals,
And there'll be no ride to freedom
Without the need to fill the searching questions,
They'd be a surplus of hollow answers
Wisdom can't attain from failure's lessons,
Innocence trapped with no enhancement
Without the battle of a personal duel,
A solitary call to arms
The spoils won't glisten like morning dew,
In flush meadows of peace and calm
Without the erroneous sea of hate,
There can be no ocean of love
There'd be no soak in seismic waves,
Amorous spells cast from above
If there's no particular urgency,

Plodding through with stagnant mind
The clock will soon be done with ticking,
And they'll be no sands of time!

Lament for the Phoenix
Scot A. Buffington

No swift consummation from ashes of past
nor set conflagrations which prophecies cast
eternal rebirthings bereft mortal tears
risings accursed, each five hundred years.

Beg for these cinders, next fortunate winds
consciously scatter on myrrh-scented sins
return to the blessings of ultimate deaths
upon solar altars that witnessed last breaths.

This Phoenix is hopeful to no longer rise
shatter existence his sapphire eyes
each reanimation from carbon to gold
weakened the heartening, heaven did hold.

Birds immemorial lived for the sky
never resented the promise to die
even as freedom flew fleeting from life
knew only one instant of soul-killing strife.

Eclipse
R. David Fletcher

Like a thief in the sudden night,
The sky god charts your doom;
Steals your mind and dims your sight
In the day of the marauding moon.

Nobody
Lana Martin

nobody's designed to take this flight
to the next level of human escapade
turning everlasting peace into a fight
and flowers' bleeding stem into a blade.

cloning the presence of God's voice
in the ultimate waste of human mind
in a skeleton of every forbidden choice
in a consciousnesses, too unrefined.

while barking the reasons of today
the pack is disclosing all their lies
got lost in the elevator of the Bay
expanding horizons in disguise.

nobody's designed to deal with the greed
of the few that need an intervention
some might think we have agreed
to all the brain holes and their pretention.

Crimson River
Valerie Dohren

A crimson river, labyrinthine flows
Down streams traversing sinister terrains
And onwards drifts along the path of life
Through myriad courses, rivulets, and veins
Along a way that takes it to the heart
Then on to where the ring of love remains

A crimson river weaving through your mind
That twists and turns one billion-fold therein
To search out all the feelings that you feel
Plus all the memories that lie within
To raise a train of thought that is sublime
Of dreams, imagination set to spin

Everything Falls Apart
Roger Simpson

One thing I know
That always happens
Is that everything falls apart
Infinitesimally
Ever so gradually
Yes, everything falls apart

Over the years
Entropy wins
And everything falls apart
I try to stand still
In calendar times
Still everything falls apart

I make it brand new
But nothing prevents
The way everything falls apart
Even memory fails
In my knotted brain
As everything falls apart

A Poem—Fox
James Alexander Crown

I take the night's air softly seeking,
Dreams held in my dreamer's keeping.
Dreams of realms beyond this plane,
Dreams I dreamt of once again.

I bridge the gap between two worlds.
My liminality unfurls
The scrolls upon which poets writ
Tales on cunning, tales of wit.

I take the night's air all a-roaming
O'er tangled woodlands all a-gloaming,

I seek the scent of the brown hare,
I seek the spoor held in the air.

I bridge the gap 'twixt There and Here,
Divest yourself of mortal fears,
I'll lead you by my vixen's wiles
Unto the dreams the earth reviles.

I take the night's air softly seeking,
Dreams held in my dreamer's keeping.
Dreams of realms beyond this plane,
Dreams I dreamt of once again.

The Silver Lake
Rufus Daigle

The silver lake of oceans grain
Like a flossed bullet
In the shell of the rising sun
Emerald waves basting in
The current of lava
Your hair splayed on pillows of
Clouds
Burnt bridges of yesterday's kiss
Just the wain of thunder
Before the climb
Your ears waxed in the tweed
Of honeycombs
Who would know how roads
Bind the hair in cuffs of your
Delicate thoughts as
The mirror runs
You finished with the prosper of the cove
Do we find wisdom at the end of the straw
Or at the beginning of the whole?
The dream is a golden sphere of galaxies
Blended in the cosmic loom of
Your passion

Mercury

Ryan Morgan

Rush-rush-rush.
Hurtling around my groove.
Push! Push! Push!
A spring overwound, I move
Expending all my energy
Circling another, more grand.
Caught in its gravity.
Harnessed to its demands.
I run around my rut
With exhausting speed,
Bound to the gamut
Of another's enthralling need.

Forbidden from slowing my pace, I race
In a ceaseless churn.
Can't avert my face from their embrace,
Within which I freeze and burn
At the same time;
Captured in a relationship
Where I'm only able to shine
In my partner's blazing grip.

Sometimes I'm forced to such swiftness
That it looks like I'm going in reverse.
It's a form of sadistic regress
To be made retrograde as you traverse.
From afar, the view may seem exciting,
But it's only the same old gyrations,
And I'll just continue to tightly spin
In increasingly quiet desperation.
The day will come when I incinerate
In this overbearing bond.
Until then I'm fated to accelerate,
Too small and scared to abscond.

The Strange Sympathy of Pendulums and Fireflies

Joseph Gallagher

Someone in the sixteenth century,
A maker of metronomes
A patron of pendulums
Observed the constant consonance of clocks
Enclosed in glass boxes...
Even those with inconsistent cadences
Eventually marched in steps of lock.

In the same way discordant metronomes
Became synchronized,
The fireflies of Southeast Asia
And the Smokey Mountains drape
Their ethereal landscapes like jewelled crepe
In a cohesive luminous dance of light and dark.

The fireflies undulating spark
Is susceptible to lithium bulbs and neon lights,
Buzzing cities transistors turned to stark
Bristled brightness. Fireflies become
Daylight moons to too many suns.
Their mating dance is fading before it's begun.

Both she and he neither buzz nor sing
For mates whose hopes include no rings.
Only a pale green fire encased
In translucent gold...
Shaken like morse code maracas,
An effluent desire unmatched—Behold!

Now the electric fizz of cobalt glass
Whose glare obscures...
Drowns their synonymous love
In unquiet pools of light.

Once our species wandered by dirt lanes

In pitch dark, led astray by flowers, spells,
Fairies, sprites and ancient elves...
To seek what daylights cloudless skies
Hid from humdrum unquestioning eyes,
Now sought to succumb to stranger selves
Where love and danger in equal measure hide
And fate or destiny is not yours to decide.

Now though the utter dark is dissolved
And desire, fireflies and clocks are out of sync,
Chance and mystery too have all been solved
Once we were chains in an ancient link...
Now we are codified, calculated, clinical, evolved,
We stand calcified, critical, on the edge of the brink.

I think some things can only be found lost
In the dark,
Somewhere far beyond the light
And oh my love, my love—
I am hiding here in plain sight...
Hiding from the dawn,
That is nearly now upon us.

In the Fields of the Great Golden Heart

Martin Gedge

Lie me down in feathers in the body of her grace
Beneath the Heaven halos in this sanctuary place
To sleep among the flowers bringing comfort to my soul
In bloom of all its gardens and its water fountain hole
In youth of all my innocence to wash away my pain
To feel the rush of saviours in the flavours of the rain
A shade that is my shelter from temptation of the mirror
Of that of passing shadows by the windows that I fear
In the still of bitter silence and in guidance of a prayer
My sky to fill with anger as the darkness fills the air
To stir of jealous envy bringing storms onto my door
A rope right through my anchor on a boat wreck shipped to shore

With gods on either shoulder more I'm colder in this wind
Crying out for angels spread your wings and take me in
May the might in all its beauty do his duty for my plight
That I shall shed my sorrows in tomorrow's morning light
The skin to peel the flesh and bone alone as I shall stand
To stairs from the survival to the arrival of his hand
As trees as wild and open I'm still hoping to embark
To run in fields of angels in this great and golden heart...

From Dusk To Dawn
Emile Pinet

A red sun pooling like a drop of blood,
Coagulates at the edge of darkness.
And the night swallows shadows in a flood
Black as pitch, within a seamless starkness.

A gilded moon, a pitted golden coin,
Gleams in the sky like a beacon of light.
And like flashing fireflies, twinkling stars join
Quasars and pulsars as sparks in the night.

Dawn frets like a nervous actor offstage,
Eager to outperform the rising sun.
And like a gentle breeze rippling the page
Morning shimmers like a web freshly spun.

Sol rises up as a scarlet balloon,
Afloat on the air like a songbird's tune.

Unplugged Harpsichord
Peter Rivers

My breath it burns like winds of scorn
Eye flown disdain, instant mind malaise
Palm percussion, golf clap of your sarcasm horn
Everything built must crumble and raze

Waves cascade, crashes upon trembling shores
What is profound intellect devoid of wisdom?
Always screaming passcodes at a handless door
Just a library, hoarding stacks, no filing system

Oh, sweet melody of soundless symphony
Alas, just a refreshing taste of arid delight
Two hearts beating in reflective synchrony
Trapped in reverberating verse, building spite

The gravity, attractive pressure to crush
Hit me, taste the bite of savage thorn
I fold, to win I needed a straight flush
If I was a victor, perhaps no scorn was ever born

Right Here
Lonnie Budro

My poet pulled up beside me
And then he yelled, "Get in!"

He smiled, and revved his engine up
And said "Let's take her for a spin."

So I sat down and I closed the door
But I began to smile in fear

These are the times, that're hard to find
These times, like these, right here

New Life
Sarah Wheatley-Tillbrook

In my true commune to nature
I have not a wound nor suture
Buried bold

Committed to a time of fracture
Cast of sin, my soul enraptured
I grew old

Placed within an iron casket
I fell strong to bread and basket
Learnt my place

Denied not my want of living
Higher voice allowed forgiving
Saved my grace

Is it us
George Valler

Take down the pen, write up the world
let's chapter the book of today
We can burn the clouds with our carbon
cut down the rings of the old forest tree
in genius we are the overriding
we will put paid to all we can see
we'll beat our chests when floods are upon us
dance a jig as the storms now roam free
clap our hands at the raging inferno
show contempt for the whole boiling sea
let the warming send flames through our forests
burn the life way out of us all
for we are the man among many
nature's own that made us stand tall
so let nature now try to destroy
for we are above and beyond
contempt for all is our middle
so go destroy and all will be gone.

Tipping the Scales
Martin Gedge

Coming down the pipe bringing a million pounds of pain
Riding like the wind on this devil dieselled train
A Cajun steel of reckless running fuel to every vein
Where angels have no mercy when the fury has the reign
A fire breathing dragon with the eyes of burning coal
Black as the unholy reaping solely on its goal
With blood rush to the temple and to dwell of every hole
To drain of the apostle as to fossil stone the soul

The breath to hath no patience of the innocence of light
To darken all the heavens with the seven serpents right
To tear upon the skin of flesh and sin and Grimm of flight
Release the storm in battle form to saddle up and fight
No man has seen the face that will in place reside the throne
To come from dark of shadows like the rattle of thy bone
The gate from deep in slate to consummate this planet dome
To leave of nothing worth as deep the earth and birth of home

And boils of the ocean rage of motion cage of fear
Quakes to shake this mountain in this fountain atmosphere
From valley deep down alley lava galley to appear
In waves beyond the skies on high to die then disappear
For human kind of lessen mind in time of such concern
The god of voice has left no choice to hoist and let it burn
To fade to dust in winds of gust combust to rust and churn
That of this fate we hesitate still apes too late to learn…

Consolations
Terry Bridges

Our needs are few
Yet we yearn for new
Time after time

Unsatisfied
By what's inside
Time after time

Fishing in pods
We summon our gods
Time after time

Solitary souls
Gathering in shoals
Time after time

Company sought
Happiness bought
Time after time

Longing for love
The universe above
Time after time

Thoughts accelerate
Through pearly gates
Time after time

Metaphysical dances
The night advances
Time after time

Down in the gutter
We slink and mutter
Time after time

The sky abounds

Deep space surrounds
Time after time

We buy our goods
The volume floods
Time after time

Nothing consoles
Changes or evolves
Time after time

We seek the pure
Black night's allure
Time after time

Into the stark
Ancestral dark
Time after time

Waking to dawn
Glad though forlorn
Time after time

Such bliss in this
The morning's kiss
Time after time

August of the Purple Hearts
Mike Absalom

It's August now, half spent.
August of the purple hearts and all flowers dressed imperial.
I threw coins down into the stones,
down there where the Black Brook flows dark as Guinness
out of the Beyond and into my small portion.
Like milk from the Black Cow's udder,
it bears away the sad present
into a paltry oblivion.

It is all-peace at first glance, here by the brock-black stream.
Scabious and Loosestrife and the Holy Saffron of the Water Margin,
monk-robed, breathing out the grasses like floral prayers.

And where the wild Vetch quilts spread and dry,
ragged rugs ageing on an Oriental highway,
Peacock Butterflies in their overblown embroidery
squeeze in among the veins of silver weed,
like tardy UFOs caught red-handed crossing the road.

A sweet opium sea of Meadowsweet breaks into surf
and sprays drought throughout the summer turlough,
spreading dark and grotesque dreams into
the unschooled willow-brakes of no-man's-land.
Fifteen years ago I set up my easel here on a knapweed bank
and right away the Wind unbuttoned all my ambitions
and sent me reeling back into an Older Place.

It's another August now, dying slowly, as we are.
August of the purple hearts and all flowers faded imperial.
I have often thrown offerings here, down into the stones
in this enchanted place where the Black Brook flows
dark as Guinness
out of the Beyont and into my Small Portion.
Like Milk from the Black Cow's udder,
it bears away the sad present into a grim forgetfulness.

Over this bóithrín violence hangs like mist.

Wild men lurk among the shades of the hill fort,
lying unseen by day, and at night low beneath the moonless
blackthorn tangle.

There are cunningly carved arrowheads in among the shards and
buttercups,
lost rubble of the Age-old Generations.
In my time coltsfoot has torn up the tarmac,
but the knapweed buttons still hold
the Holy Rainbow snapdragon closed.

This is an empty place today: it's only me and the Cows.
But if you pause a moment and look past the hill fort,
MacAdam and MacEve are still here!
And because this has never stopped being Paradise,
and because Hell is never far away,
they are both still looking for an Antidote to the Apple…

…and so am I!

Ghost Town
Martha M. Miller

The swings in the park
move with an absent wind,
empty.
The sun, through the watching skeletons
of abandoned buildings
and the glowing haze of fog,
paints shadows of children
who once played here
on the ground,
like the echoes of laughter
now mimicked by the birds
with the scratching scurry
of the rats
through the detritus
of a newly ghosted town.

Monet

Joseph Gallagher

I believe the notion of fidelity
Is less true in painting
Than in marriage.
How can we assemble light,
Traveling from a star to some wisteria
Purple upon a bridge overgrown with green
Between them, the midday sun sashays
Like my fleet scattering brush...
Nothing solid stays.

That which I gaze upon has disappeared.
I hear the low lapping of the water
Upon the lily pad.
The sound is similar to the vibration
That limns the water's edge
Into blurred fragments of blue.

Within the river's reflection,
The riddle of line and light remains a question
That will be restored by the water's motion...
My 'cat's tongue' brushes lapping
The paradox of movement upon this canvas
Even these cataracts shall not cloud my vision.

What I see is diffuse.
The halo in the fog of city streetlights,
The gas lamps have filaments
That wave like Angel's wings.
The world is fluid. Light dissolves
Becoming whatever it touches...

Melding sky and sea, rain and rivers
Anointed, caressed by my four brushes.
If this brush were a violinist's bow...
These whirling notes like auditory sparks
Would wash upon your ears
With a wildness that would break your heart.

Quiet, Mon Amour
Jessica Ferreira Coury Magalhães

Quiet, mon amour
The city is asleep
The streets are all obscure
The clouds above just slowly creep.

Quiet, mon amour
This is the hour for lovers to weep
Dies an old day...adieu, vieux jour
Along with the secret it keeps.

Quiet, mon amour
I want to hear your heartbeat
Feel the heat of your body, your allure
In the silence, love is so sweet.

Refrain
Linda Falter

How loud is the silence?
My tears are all dry
How full is empty?
My mind wonders why
How long is always?
My heart wants to know
How can I stay, when I have to go?
My soul is a spirit
How can you not hear it?
My memories remain
How come I also, feel the pain?
My life is a mystery
How can you explain?
My lips kiss your lips
How good the refrain
We are ....soulmates
One and the same....

Poetry Geist

Patrick Darnell

Tell the water to be still
Call the clouds if you will
Tell light to sit tight,
Tell time to stop ...
... on a dime

Tell those who pray ...
... to call it a day
When you feel ignored
Don't blame the Lord
Doesn't sound cricket
Worms with rickets
On a pitch field of dreams
Being so thick, they
Sully the stream.

To think, to even stir,
Required eternal dirge,
To stop and say
In turn, true to form,
Someone out there
Invented this—

Beside the stillness in shade,
Individuals fell against, afraid,
The high ranging tidal wave
The poetry geist had made.

static spring
Matt Elmore

as yesterday smiles on tomorrow's flowers
joys spring upon sorrows today!
sweet moments cling, pollinating the sour
as yesterday smiles on tomorrow's flowers
arranging encouragers with less doubters
hope clings to that freshest bouquet
as yesterday smiles on tomorrow's flowers
joys spring upon sorrows today!

Quicksand
David Catterton Grantz

You ask my leave to pile your gold,
You, the blight of haters, bold,
Planting spite and retribution,
Within the dead-eyed Lilliputian.

What's good for all escapes the grasp
Of everyone who bolts his lasp,
For smears and jeers cement their loss,
As fear brings anguish to its cross.

Their tumult oozing from the slime
Would drag us backward to a time
When power absent righteousness
Consumed us in divisiveness,

Imploding the very citadels
Built to transcend public hells;
High treason's wasps buzz out his call,
Their tyrant building tall his wall.

His bile has found the mind's quicksand,
As kindness slips away, as planned.

Ghost of Winter Past

Charlene Phare

Lamented winds through bare trees blast
Multicoloured leaves lay abandoned
Just skeletal ghosts of winter past

Sprinkled sugar mountains that last
Frosty morns grate like shards of sand
As lamented winds through bare trees blast

Dark afternoon clouds, the die is cast
Sunlight lowered from her hand
Another ghost of winter past

Cold reception no response from mast
Glaciers formed on the wasteland
As lamented winds through bare trees blast

Swollen shadows struck too fast
Consumed like stolen contraband
Forgotten ghosts of winter past

Forgiveness is all that we can ask
After all nothing goes as planned
Lamented winds through our bare trees blast
We're skeletal ghosts of our winters past

Loneliness

Karen Bessette

Where do I go now that you are gone from me? loneliness
has murdered me slowly. I find myself staring now at
strangers, trying to see their hearts. Holding on to daylight,
afraid to dream, afraid not to. Is love a madness or is
loneliness?

Anvil of the Mind
Steve Wheeler

He shimmers
in the lucid lilac haze
and fading recollections
of a grand, illustrious time
when blind simplicity awoke
the innocence of minds.

Now dimming
in a pallid parting daze
he lays those strange confections
on the anvil of the mind;
There, quiet dualities evoke
in everything he finds.

Slow glimmers
in his quickening twilight gaze
light up belovéd reflections
of the circles he defined,
of all he loved and all he spoke
into God's arms consigned.

he died
Deborah Griffin Howard

into my dreams
of another life
in between
he died
and left me
into my dreams

Lift Her Up

Natasha Browne

Lift her up,
Up to the moon,
Like the flowers lift up,
When they bloom.

Fill her cup,
So she can soar,
With the eagles,
To explore.

Lift her high,
Into the sky,
Like a parent,
Lifts a child.

Then she'll grow wings,
Like a light feathered bird,
She'll lift you up with her,
With ought saying a word.

She'll catch you if you fall,
She won't complain at all,
She'll let you rise,
Higher than her in the sky.

She'll take care of you for life,
Then become your wife,
Or your friend,
Until the end.

Lift her up,
So she can catch you,
Catch her,
As she'll lift you up too.

My Own Chains
Martin Gedge

Wrapped into this mayhem in this metal mortal coil
My temperature is rising as my skin begins to boil
This heart is much too heavy on this leavy that I stand
A minuscule of morsel as a measurement of man
In air to wince a weasel fighting for a catch of breath
While demons dealing punctures in the pores that I have left
The dark and dingy shadows are proceeding on my fear
While a slow and fading vision in condition gathers near
There is no place of refuge and no grace to save my soul
But a grip as tight as night to swallow light and bite me whole
In penance for my past I will not last to see the day
For no pity for the old too lay there cold and to decay
A show to meet the eyes in this disguise defies the norm
A throne to sit a fool while spitting drool into the storm
I have not much of words for clergy herds of peaceful prayer
No mercy of the court as to abort but stop and stare
For one hand upon the trigger not much bigger than the fuse
A meal to seal the deal how does it feel just when you lose
I'll gladly take the charge a volt as large to cleanse my pain
For all the sorrow that I borrow no tomorrow I remain….

A Pink and Blue Sky
Emile Pinet

Dawn pierces the dark at first light
as flocks of mourning doves take flight.
And although the sky seems so stark
at first light, Dawn pierces the dark.

Sol liquefies like molten gold,
it's incredible to behold.
For just as the sun starts to rise,
like molten gold, Sol liquefies.

Darkness flees into the shadows

77

like a merging murder of crows.
And as birds abandon the trees,
into the shadows, darkness flees.

Colors intensify with light,
sunlight superseding moonlight.
And inking a pink and blue sky,
with light; colors intensify.

watching
Deborah Griffin Howard

the window of my soul
watching until
the sun goes down
watching you
for you are the one
who is watching me
from above

giving me a sacred bow
feeling like you understand

never will I celebrate
all the hate that comes for me
for I am ready to love you
unconditionally

watching
for all of us
waiting until
the sun goes down

Life in the Key of E
William Fields

bridges of hearts from generations past
pierces flesh that embodies your soul
and the spirit lays claim to a missionary
zeal that ignites paths which fosters the goal

while being third place on the C major scale
shan't hinder your quest for light
its valiant attempt is dwarfed by a measure
which portions harmonious plight

but off key rhythms from tumultuous cries
through shutters of a motionless ship..
will falter what's meant for new wine
into wineskins that's served from the cup that we'd sip

yet as smiles brought to laughter paired with
struggle and tears gifts a feast that's prepared with decree
we'll rejoice in the moment when inhaled
what's bestowed living life in the key of E

Baby
Michael Hislop

Newborn sun
Bursting into bright
In instant light
I Am exclaimed
In a giant breath
Ahhhh
Suckling on stardust
Blinking cosmic rays
Spectra revealing
Mother
She Universe
Sprawling Her embrace

Cradling gigantic arms
Baby
Mmmmm
I shall name Him
Star
Her love echoing
Everywhere as subtle waves

We Had the Hours
Becky Topham

Sometimes I think that is you I see
At the turn of this leafy street
That beloved walk and tilt of head
And there is a skip in my heart's beat

Sometimes I think that it is you I hear
Laughing in the shifting breeze
Or is it your silhouette passing soundlessly
Between the silver trunk of trees?

Sometimes I think I could touch you
Link my arm—familiar—through yours
Cling to you when the weather is wild
And the wind screams and roars

Sometimes I think that I feel you
The benevolence of your heart
And I wonder, do you remember—
That I was there at its start?

Always I wish for just one more hour
I would give almost anything
Just to touch the apple of your cheek again
My beautiful raven-haired twin

We had the hours
We weren't gifted any more
Fate came and stole you from me
Though it may not steal what went before

Throwing Boots
Chuck Porretto

Do horses throw boots at a stake in the ground?
Are boisterous ponies just boying around?
Do gossiping cats let the child out the bag?
Would a raven be bro-ing, when wanting to brag?

If a kitty can't speak, did a kid get its tongue?
Are chickens spring ladies when they're very young?
Does an unlucky snake roll a pair of man eyes?
If a stag has no date, is he showing up guy?

Do they play boy, boy, girl, at a party for ducks?
Do rabbits think people feet bring them good luck?
Does a rat on the job join the Sapien race?
And do geese often go on a wild people chase?

The Embers of Old Souls
Archie Papa

We could marvel in our likeness for a lifetime
glimmers of starlight in our children's eyes
or hate our differences until death finds us
and remorse forever whispers our goodbyes

We could share precious time we have captured
with memories of family and friends
or let greed steal trinkets appeasing the future
burdening love to forgive the evil fear defends

We could find a way to join our paths of life
an innocence again seen in our eyes
or turn oneself away into the shadows
in darkness, truth is nothing more than lies

An ancient time delivered us from stardust
aloft in winds of time we shall return
as only light, we'll shine in our likeness
until the embers of old souls no longer burn

81

Logic
Karin J. Hobson

It came to me in vision's eye a thought of premise in being seen;
For who am I to speak and answer whys
When only Eternity answers?

A perfume bottle on a stand awaiting usage from the hand;
So, too, is the mind at rest awaiting stir from heaven's bequest;
Do we simply wander-by thinking of our lives?
Do we question or reply in the breath we take each day?
For what is crack in a roof,
if leak comes in and hits as proof upon your head,
Soaking thru
And, yet you stand unawares?
Hold true to you who speaks these words,
And with logic works with heart
The every meaning of a voice from the past to mornings start.

Red Rose Blood
Jenni Nichols

Roses,
sweet and intoxicating,
wither,
crushed and destroyed...
barbs,
wretchedly impaling my heart
with melancholy darkness...
Thorny tresses,
invade deep inside my marrow,
wrapping around sinews,
piercing me with sadness.

Red rose blood seeps,
between the cracks
of my soul...

Beyond This Moment

Lana Martin

volcanic drops welded our dreams tonight
although tired from hot metal and wire,
the eruption of narcissistic hatred and spite,
provoked our visions to go on fire.

the dreams made of sorrowful barb wire
leaning at the door burnt down to ash
dusty winds of darkness in a light attire
with our values and visions harshly clash.

we wonder whether we'll always see
this door that defends our deep insides
sheltering lights within which all are free
where darkness to angels softly confides.

Aurora

Lorna McLaren

She danced across the late night sky
in petticoats of vivid hue,
a wondrous sight to please the eye
for those who had the chance to view.
Her undulating skirts entrance,
a cosmic treat of pure delight,
as technicolour swathes enhance
the beauty of this ethereal flight.
Then as she's ending her display
the colours then will start to wane,
no more to be seen of her ballet,
Aurora leaves as quietly as she came.

What the Dickens

Chuck Porretto

I was quoting Mr. Dickens
and divining Mr. Drood,
when a pompous Mr. Bigguns
with a critic's dour mood;
would declare between his sippin'
of a tepid red Bordeaux;
"I have heard you reference Dickens,
I have seen you mention Poe."

Then he lectured through his glasses
that were hanging off his nose;
"I have taught a thousand classes,
I have volumes of their prose.
I am tenured, I'm positioned,
I am qualified to know.
You shall never be a Dickens,
you shall never be a Poe."

I could feel my fingers twitchin'
and my nape could feel the hair;
as my demons felt an itchin'
for a franker form of fare.
So I loosened up my collar,
and I slowly leaned his way;
then I whispered to the scholar.....
..... "You are right in what you say.

I shall never be a Dickens,
I shall never be a Poe.
I'll not even be a Whitman,
Dostoevsky or Thoreau.
And the deviation thickens
when their brilliance starts to glow,
for I'm not as good as Dickens,
and I'm not as good as Poe.

How I wish I was their equal,
how I wish I was their heir;
but I'll never be the sequel,
to that literary pair.
I'm not even in the pickin'
at the local talent show;
even though they are not Dickens,
even though they are not a Poe.

I would love to be a Faulkner,
I would love to be a Twain.
Could you love me as a Charlotte,
or an Emily or Jane?
Oh, the joy to be a Melville
or a Dumas or Dafoe;
even more to be a Dickens,
even more to be a Poe.

I'm no Homer. That's a given;
being Hemingway is hard.
And I'll never be as driven
as the great Immortal Bard.
No more Virgils to be minted,
seldom Sophocles on stage.
No more Dantes to be printed,
or Cervantes on the page.

But I need not be a Milton,
and I need not be a Joyce;
for the windmills I am tiltin'
is a predetermined choice.
As my vitals, they will quicken
as I'm tiltin' to a fro;
though I dare not tilt with Dickens,
or be pitted 'gainst a Poe.

Yes, I'll never be a Kipling,
and I'll never be a Frost;
but it need not be so crippling,

that I'm feeling all is lost.
So I'll follow my convictions
when my ink begins to flow;
even though I'm not a Dickens,
even though I'm not a Poe.

Oh I'll never sound like Tolkien,
and I'll never look like Verne;
Even if I smell the smokin'
when my fingers feel the burn.
But my roux it never thickens
like a Franklin or Rousseau.
Though I love the feel of Dickens,
and I love the touch of Poe.

So although I'm not a Dickens,
and although I'm not a Poe;
I won't countenance depictions
from your ivory minstrel show.
You may file your sage convictions
in the place they ought to go....
...in the hole below your Dickens,
nestled deep within your Poe.

And your taunts will never tempt me,
for alas, they're so much bull;
with your journal ever empty,
and your mouth that's ever full.
You don't get to count my chickens,
with your raven but a crow;
I shall treat you as the Dickens....
...... just be glad it isn't Poe."

So Soon

Carl Gomez

So soon
The pink blossoms fade and fall
But this is a prelude
To the summer sun's fiery call
Tongues of leaves will renew

And
Already budding is autumn's fruit
Swelling through fat summer's rays
Purple and green is spring's suit
Sustained by the rain of winter's days

And I
Will pass this way at start of day
Not seeing your dusty, smoky coat
Instead it will be blossom in my eye
And memory of Spring's first, sweetest note

unhappy hour

Matt Elmore

immersed in poetry without one word
a brood of vipers congregating toothless
sees a distorted image of what used to be
gross reflections of hypocrisy once heavenly
running makeup beautifying abominations
lost in ideals of hope laughter and family
blurred by prayers of hopeless drunks alone
drinking to silent mirrors behind raised bars
never looking one another in watery eyes
for fear that fluid insecurities be revealed
immersed in poetry without one word

pour on, oh bartender of empty upper room
whisper soul cocktails of stirred golden grails

relieve me wrecked in unseen solitary reveries
junk arm jukebox croak on today's slow woes
drain what remains of overtime recollections
wretched work finished forever to be continued
simply to keep uncaring registers clanging
drunk off elixirs of intoxicating experiences
now swollen of head, sick to shrunken stomach
swaying to broken beats of this broken home
immersed in poetry without one word

Don't Grieve Too Long
Valerie Dohren

Don't grieve too long my darling
There's a world where flowers grow
And you have tarried much too long
Veiled by the crystal snow.

Don't linger in the twilight
Where the darkness clouds your mind—
Return to where the sky is bright
Boundless and unconfined.

Don't be afraid my darling
To go where the children play
Below the burnished golden sun—
Walk in the light of day.

Don't grieve too long my darling
In a place where life is done—
Behold the splendour of the world
Dancing beneath the sun.

Proxima Centauri

Ryan Morgan

After the emptiness of space
We can rest in a new place,
Our thundering night-run done,
Under a bright, unsullied sun.
The journey's length
Strained our strength
As we scraped off our history
To achieve escape velocity.

Leaving attachment and shame,
An eager itching yen for fame,
The ice and fire
Of enticement and desire,
And conflict's stiff, savage grin
So addictive to indulge in.

We rejected nostalgia and regret,
And our propensity to forget,
The unbidden touches
Of our hidden impulses,
And the shearing breath
From fearing death.

We weaved through the scree
Of fields strewn with debris;
The tough spots, sharp bends,
Flying by the rough odds and ends
Into the chaos which has ever grown
Where we cross over into the unknown.

Dreaming, we traversed the empty void,
Keeping to our course and barely buoyed
By the prospect of heady hope,
We directed our telescope,
Orienting our vessel to a new, lustrous star;
Radiant, special and so wondrously far.

With courage and steel,
By touch, by feel,
Intuition and dead reckoning
Toward the new sun ahead, beckoning
With its singing bliss of light,
Through the nothingness of night.

After calculation and divination
We come to station at our destination.
Rare worlds of wonder
Are unfurled to discover.
Perhaps here we can
Adhere to a new plan.
Refashion our natures,
Feel compassion in our labours.
Be more the angel, and less the ape
In this strange, alien, fresh landscape.
A new chance at salvation
Away from the influence of damnation.
For our souls we can yet save
If we are bold, respectful and brave.

But I'm still me, unfortunately.
I carry the debris of history.
I hope I can shed
The grip of its dead,
Weighted hand,
Before it's too late to land.

I Wonder Why
David Simpson

Nuclear power—
I wonder why,
When there's
A free reactor,
In the sky.

Chatbot Blues

Steve Wheeler

I don't ever want to write
Like ChatGPT-3
If you ever find me doing so
Please drop me in the sea
And if I start to churn out
Any soulless cliched rhymes
Dispatch me to the wilderness
For my literary crimes

Oh ChatGPT-3
You're a travesty to me
Just stay away from poetry
Don't try to be
What you can't be
You never will a poet be
Just ChatGPT-3

If my poetry descends into
A bland and hackneyed mess
With rhyming couplets forced
Into a facile pool of sess
Please save me from such drivel
Put me out of my misery!
Cos I don't ever want to write
Like ChatGPT-3

No I don't ever
Want to ever
Write like ChatGPT-3

April Nocturne

Terry Bridges

The silence purrs in the dark
Cracked light glows then disappears
Memories shout out at me...bark
Through my ancient antique years

There's wonder in the thunder
The deaf roar of quiet evenings
A moon splits night's sky asunder
Many images...many meanings

It's almost summer how I feel
Not disconsolate or sad
I pray in awe as I kneel
For the good times and the bad

Days slip through grasping fingers
Like slow sifting grains of sand
Some goes to waste...but hope lingers
Treasure stored in hearts...contraband

Symbiosis

Tom Cleary

To live life well learn to suffer pain
for knowing only pleasure is but half.
The nodes of both exist together chained
and were not Nature's impulse or a gaffe.
They breathe as twins, as day and night depend
on one another, balancing the flow
so together bring a skilful blend—
sensation heightened, helping us to grow.

House of Fire
Roger Simpson

I will live in a house of fire
I will sleep in a bed of flames
Burn those memories so bitter
Burn burn burn those aching names

See the future burning brightly
See the past is turned to ash
I don't need your dirty money
Make a bonfire of your cash

Can you see the flash of lightning?
Can you see the tiger's eyes?
By the light of honest fires
We will clean up all your lies

I will live a life of burning
I will breathe the red hot air
See combustion do it's good work
See the flames show how they care

See the conflagration rising
Feel the searing cleansing heat
Fuel the fire with useless longing
At one with purity so sweet

Lunch
Robert Speights

Sit and stare
Among the fields
Your presence there
My spirit yields

The green of earth
Touching blue
Since rebirth
Draw close to you

93

Staring off
To in-between
Where the cross
Was stood and seen

Jesus Christ
The middle ground
Two worlds spliced
The act profound

Of time and space
He is the center
God's human face
The way to enter

Through the veil
To His throne
Good news to tell
How grace was shown

Now, the present
Life offering
Hands to plow
Our hearts we bring

What if William Shakespeare had written a technical guide to blockchain technology?
Chris Brew

Its soul a mage has carved from one and none.
From light's fleet rushing substance is it made
What is said is said, what is done is done
The acts of those who would their dues evade
Block by block it serves to bind and chain //
Impartial judge impanelled in a lock
That when once opened, none can close again
The chains that bind are hidden in this block //

So now, no king his oaths can freely break
No prince his trusted promises disdain
Or for his own or for another's sake //
We'll not contract and calculate in vain
But this, unless the leopard change his spots
Is poisoned hemlock for my weaker plots

Find the Light
Peter Rimmer

Follow the honeyed road
As sun sets over sea
Nightfall wears a cloak of stars
Choose one as Earth turns
Night to day.

Find the light
In morning time
Wear it with reverence
Light of day
Kiss of grace
This brief interlude
An eternity.

Distance
Archie Papa

Graffiti in the reflection
a glare up in the sky
a shadow almost center stage
of a lonely passerby

Homes along the horizon
shops on the edge of town
clouds of golden glory hang
above her like a crown

And as the lazy river
will follow its own pace
light will cast a divine spell
on all those in its grace

Here a glance is captured
from a moment time set free
and long may it now travel
remembered by you and me

Catching Up To Your Mistake
Eric Aguilar

Catching up to your mistake
is like finding land once lost at sea.
There is no misconception of the
mirage meant to mislead, for your truth
is now standing firm on solid ground.
By the loosened arrow, inaccuracy gives
way to the measure of the target, therefore
further adjustments are of course.

Catching up to your mistake is as
a bridge over changing water,
the tax and toll are a personal price.
The mistake is an oversight that gives
a clear vision of once-blurry beliefs.
The snafu of confusion precursors clarity.

Catching up to your mistake
is like a flight of stacked stairs;
the mighty fall of a misstep is
related to the balance of poise.
To get past the mistake, you must
commit to one step at a time.

Catching up to your mistake is
the indifference of real and true.

A false move has to navigate around
the tremendous terrain of truth;
thereby, giving a legend to the map.

Adapt at the faux pas and
go past your misconceptions.
Catching up to your mistake, at
best is a beauteous badge earned,
for what is knowledge worth
less there be lessons learned.

Dropped Luggage
Charlene Phare

I dropped your luggage down the hallway
I watched it go through the chute
I saw your face go through the motions
I saw your mind try to compute

I heard your pennies falling
I felt the pain you felt
I couldn't hear you calling
My heart refused to melt

I froze the time we spent
I found fond memories
I papered over our cracks
I had to take my leave

I dropped your luggage down the hallway
I watched as you waved goodbye
I'm never turning around again
There's nothing to see in my eye

Your Story

Jamie Willis

I read you at first glance.
Blue eyes cannot hide much.
Cool and bright, soft and light...
But no mystery inside.

I don't make the rules, but I will break each one
A lawless lover loving love like leaving's not a lasting loss
I sipped your words and turned your page
Then gave you a careless toss.

Predictable does not mean safe
While greener grass grows in the wild
And if safety is in numbers, there's a worn out,
Well-read pile of tales as old as I am
Where the lies are all the same, and the wants
Are all so basic and the tropes are dull and tame.

I need a thrill.

Your eyes reflect the sky. The water, too, a saccharin blue
A pleasant preset placed upon a vast but mostly empty space.

Blood and guts and tears and pasts, and passion's fingers
Carving paths, and haunted harrowed tales of night
And sweat soaked songs of champion fights ...
The scars and wrecks and broken bones
And broken hearts and broken homes...
The blush of bearing dark disgrace,
The times of meeting ego's face...

I'll read that book. I'll take my time.
I'll cherish every single line.
I'll draw it out inside my mind and savor every brilliant bite.

Don't waste me on your baby blues and on your story's vapid hues.
If on rainy days your eyes go grey, or jealousy brings jaded shade...
When you have something real to say...
I'll be the first to read your book that day.

To Sail the Sky

Gregory Richard Barden

cast tie-lines to shadowy depths above
meteors to plunge the ocean of suns
kick off—tally-ho! from the pier of known
a scoundrel's nod to the skull and bone

vast skies uncharted now beckon ahead
a dusk of dreams splashed yellow and red
naught but astounding, the adventures be
an endless sojourn 'cross a sparkling sea

the sky-palette waits for a score of tales
come a warm solar wind to puff the sails
all worries and why's now, abaft the beam!
set our course due for a foolish dream!

a celestial tempest to bend the jack
to his tasking a-hold the kicking strap
stem the tide, aye, mind the moonbeam drift
spread her wings wide and give her lift

the sextant's now set to the Milky Way
(we'll grave her clean on a windless day)
to port side, a wink from the Seven Sisters
off starboard, the gleam of nebulous vistas

we sunder the clouds with our wake of mist
now dark matter deep and heaven-kissed
tossed by the waves through a sea of night
we gasp for the void, yet we drown in light

our spirits denuded and paean-versed
we dare constellations to do their worst
for now we all pull to the labor at hand
to chart the expanse of this boundless land

at the bidding and mercy of a rapturous breeze
three prayers for fair winds and following seas

'til our hearts are sated and our marrow torn
and we drop our anchor there, worry-worn ...

on the sands of time, we'll commend our dance
and return our dust ... to the great expanse.

How Very Strange
Valerie Dohren

How strange it is, how very strange
That in the still of night
I feel the beating of my heart
Then catch the morning light
That dances on the shadowed walls
To captivate my sight.

How could I so behold the dawn
And feel such joy inside
When all the world has slipped away
And everything has died—
There's now a flicker of the flame
That I can no more hide.

It is so strange, so very strange
When filled with such dismay
That I should ever be so moved
To see the children play
And watch the falling of the sun
As at the close of day.

So strange it is, so very strange
That life yet moves along—
This world will keep revolving whilst
The chorus sings its song
And all that is will ever stay
Full resolute and strong.

Easy on Me
Martin Gedge

It came to my surprise
As she said her last goodbyes
While the tears around her eyes
they fell like rain
And in that moment in the dark
All the pain had burned a mark
And the spark that warmed her heart
Had lost its flame
For this flower once to bloom
Has got up and left this room
To live her presence with the gloom
She held so deep
When you lose your closest friend
It doesn't matter in the end
If the promise we pretend
We couldn't keep
And for the words to say in kind
To give us all some peace of mind
If we could only find the time
To let them know
It is more than just to enough
To reach out and show your love
When these angel wings of dove
As white as snow
For a life that isn't fair
We hear those whispers in the air
If you really care to share
To be sincere
Why do we wait until they're gone
Like a gnome to grace the lawn
When it took you so damn long
When I was here...

Burnt Bridges
Karin J. Hobson

The forest fire succumbs to its own temptation;
Like feral flames jumping from prey to prey;
So, too, does man and his heated anger;
Leading his everyday common sense and sanity astray;
When all is said and done to inflict,
Smoke and ashes shall clash against caches writ;
Your dealing hand massacred a tawdry gruesome grit;
Like burnt bridges compounding unsteady foot to ground;
Anguished wails outweigh flagrant flames subpoenaed to astound;
Let thine ear adhere to sagacious words spoken,
Lest repeated trumpet pursue traumatic scar as token;
Children willingly comprehend hand on stove exacts pain;
Misery's rivalling blame game only imposes further gain;
What searing Sun forced Crow to seek shade?
But, Murders request for common sense to reign;
And, so too, will stand intellectual man unfeigned.

A Journey of Broken Shards
Suzanne Newman

The broken shards of my broken life
Lay scattered across the bathroom floor,
Where the broken shards of my broken peace
Make these pilgrims' feet bleed 'til they pour,
The broken shards of my broken dreams
Have fallen in the corner's cracks,
And the broken shards of broken joy
Are covered in dust and tears of black.

I try to collect these broken shards,
That have scattered so high and scattered so far,
But as I attempt to pick them up,
My fingers, thumbs, and palms get cut.

These shards are sharp like razor-blades,
And slice so deeply from life's pain,
I look around, and simply cannot see
How these shards are of any use to me.

I fall down on the floor in pieces,
Amongst the blood and broken pieces,
Don't know why life fell to pieces,
But I pray to God to help me fix these pieces.

The Lord views me with compassionate eyes,
Because He is gracious, loving and kind,
And then my wounds He tends and binds,
And gifts me peace and hope inside.
God takes these broken shards of mine,
Holds them in His potter's hands divine,
And reassures me when He deems it's time,
He will help me make a masterpiece so fine.

Restoration and creation,
I see is possible from this devastation,
Soul and faith say I must simply trust
The one who grants me sweet salvation.

And, gradually, every broken bit
Starts to slot in place and somehow fit,
No longer injuring me with nicks,
But building a picture, through God's mosaic.

By using faithful eyes to see,
I can make vague sense of what's before me,
Not everything, but enough to see,
How the Lord is shaping and maturing me.

This restoration is still incomplete,
I'm still broken in places, head's messy not neat,
But I walk life's mosaic with pleased pilgrim's feet,
Trusting God every day 'til my journey's complete.

Things given also taken
Peter Rivers

Feel your heart, know your light
Never stop growing, chasing stars
Help others start, shining bright
Forever never knowing, secret stolen jars
Feelings fade and must depart,
Now out of sight, becoming long forgotten night…

I See the Moon
Gayle-Anne Hart

I see the moon,
And the moon sees me.
Shining down like a silver coin,
Just sitting above that tree.

I see the moon,
And the moon lights my way.
Hovering high above,
In the dark night sky.

I see the moon,
Making shadows on the ground,
Shapes long and flat,
Stretching as hours pass.

I see the moon,
And the moon sees me.
Slowly moving across the sky,
Making room for the day.

Star Rider

Ronnie Tucker

Colors explode as mind and space collide
In confusion sources awaken
Transform in moments
Illusion advances in notions
Transparent in elusive dreams

Follow the star watcher
As his gaze is fixed to the tranquility of space
Sound out to the galleons
of the transitions of time and space
Back and forth the universe,
a liquid ocean of pure ethereal splendor
Starlight illuminating the pathways

Moon glider awakens the cosmic self
As the sun-rider takes flight in the distant night
Merging as one with the distortion
Contemplating the knowledge
Of universal man

Soul watcher all seeing in his tower
As his essence awaits his return
Parallels his sights to be whole
He moves fast as his ship sails on and on
Seeker of destiny a true believer

The stars open to his destination
As so many images surround his wondering eyes
So many to contain in his view
In the rhythms and all the glory
Expanding and expanding his horizons

One speck in this sea of eternal existence
No illusion for they are real
In the songs of the planets
All is heard, all is nurtured
Clearly all is to behold in the movements

Fly pass on the way to eternity
Realms beyond all meanings
For it's all an everlasting circle
Chasing the knowledge born out of reason
In this ever changing of cosmic seasons

He is one with the universe
He is one with the systems
He is one with the stars
He is one with eternity
He is one with space and time

Performers Regret Stone
Peter Rivers

Emotionless your sad eyes kiss
So motionless, ready to dismiss
Where you'll be this sad mind sees
Standing lonely through eternities
A victor cast that good guy stare
But stranger still he's unaware
Target painted on the rise,
To no surprise
If you reach new highs,
You must cut old time ties
Easy choice, quickly made,
To cut me out
You can't fool me,
I know your insides shout
Maybe it should make you cry,
You not me, chose to say goodbye...
Maybe I was worth the try,
I'm a different kind of guy...

jinx
Matt Elmore

I looked you over
like a four leaf clover
inside your mind
I never did find
any quick closure
for you were a serious joker
smearing smiles
trading trials
rubbing raw rainbows
robbed of denials
while faded in shades
black on white
your painful delights
awaited out of sight
for when I thought I was lucky
I had lost the game
with nothing left but a memory
and a jinx for the shame

Scythes and Blades
Rufus Daigle

I tried to tell you so many times
How scythes and blades
Run bones to fire
I held you like a comet passing
Couldn't hold you more
You came with him
You left with him
I tried to tell you many times
How scythes and blades
Run bones to fire
The lines I wrote were embossed with tears
The time I gave was all I had to give
To you

The Pulse of War

E.C. McCaffrey

I hear the sound of boots approaching
The pulse of war is ever growing
The heart of man, calloused and numb
Marches to the savage drum
Vibrations of a coming battle
Can you hear the death knell rattle?

Beat by one, beat by two
Flags that wear a blood red hue
Who is left to reap the harvest?
The hour of man falls into darkness
A conquest gained by subjugation
Victory of every nation

Beat by three, beat by four
They are banging at the door
The advent of this ancient struggle
The weak will bend their knees will buckle
While profit springs from distant shores
By the gold that's made in wars

Beat by five, beat by six
The clamor of our politics
The whistling of bombs that soar
Earth is shaking at its core
The heartbeat of a fallen nation
That echoes war within creation

Beat by seven, beat by eight
The media will recreate
Blame the death of fallen men
On religion, make it a sin
While the drumbeat keeps in time
The rhythm of a voiceless crime

Beat now nine, beat now ten
The war drum sounds its call again

The pulse of men throbs like a moan
The beating of a metronome
Keeping time for what's to come
By the war cry's hollow drum

Please Remember Me
Stephen W. Atkinson

For those who sleep
From battles lost
And paid, for us,
The ultimate cost

For all who came back from war
Forever scarred by what they saw

The lucky ones,
So they say
They got to see
Another day

But friends who fell
At the toll of death's bell
Still haunt their dreams
Upon a field of screams

Where poppies now dwell
As a veil across hell
Where bones still lie
And the lost still cry:

Remember me, please!
Please, remember me!

I, in deepest earth
And I, in deepest sea

Please don't forget
Please remember me.

Silence Only I Can Hear

Gavin Prinsloo

There is a violence held within
The silence that only I can hear,
Perceived by eyes who hear no cries,
It can be a source of fear

Yet here am I but can but rely
Upon lips that do not move,
There is no time in silence sublime,
And within its quiet I move

None will know but what I show
They need not understand,
For my violence is wrapped in silence
Which lays within my hand

You do not know what words will show
Nor will you understand my cause,
I cannot speak my courage too weak
To obey those social laws

I am wrapped in a cloud my thoughts
Are loud, yet in silence I find my way,
Yet still I awake my faith
To break to live another day

So do not feel that it is not real
When my tongue does not reply,
For my lips are sealed until what was cut
Is healed, a truth I cannot deny

Yet the words you speak in times so bleak,
Do not withold nor pull apart,
For the need is the seed in the strength
Of silence to calm a broken heart

Red Feather

Dale Parsons

I'll take a plain white feather to start
Into this I will tenderly imbue
The warmth and fondness of my heart
And, all the love that it holds there for you

From white into pink, then pink into red
The feather brightens each passing day
So vivid it becomes with every memory fed
A vibrant red, that will never fade away

Now these could be my last words spoken
Though I beam a smile as they are said
So now as I pass on to you, this token
Know it was you that turned my feather red

When it's time to say my last goodbye
And the ties to my life finally sever
Please don't cry any tears for I
Just think upon...this bright red feather

I Water You, You Water Me

Carter George Rob

I water you, you water me,
Watering each other continuously.
We grow together effortlessly,
Nourishing our love for all to see.

True love blossoms gradually,
It's like magic, it's alchemy.
That's how love flows eternally,
I water you, you water me.

Life Sentences

Steve Wheeler

This life be a crazy freak show
Like a car crash shot in slo mo
First it suck and then it blow
This life be a crazy freak show

This life be a no show FOMO
Caught up in the undertow flow
Yeah as above \ yeah so below
This life be a no show FOMO

This life be a busted stop \ go
Road block with the high viz low glow
My soul just lost all of its mojo
This life be a busted stop \ go

This life be drownin' like Cousteau
Deep sunk in an ocean tableau
No status quo on the sea flo'
This life be drownin' like Cousteau

This life be like waitin' for Godot
'Sa same for U an' me both bro
No gold at the end of dis rainbow
This life be like waitin' for Godot

This life be a knock-off Merlot
Shot down by a store-door hobo
Smashed bottle next to a John Doe
This life be a knock-off Merlot

But I ain't gonna call it no MOF
No you ain't gonna see me stoop so low
Because that was never my M.O.
This life be a crazy freak show

I Stand Tall
Graeme Stokes

A malevolent tsunami, the frenzied waves, come crashing in!
Pounding at ailing bastion, the scrutinisation begins
Probing for holes in my shattered ego, imploring capitulation
I engage each desperate muscle and sinew, conscious of isolation
A breath of hope my scanty barrier, strength of will my shield
I draw upon my last reserves; to the darkness, I do not yield!

Hissing poison at my psyche, with its vitriolic bile
A spitting, vile, rabid foam, impatient to defile
It's craving all there's ever been, covets every locked in scene
Every dear and distant memory, those forever lost at sea
The voices beg for subjugation, waves interrogate ever harder!
To divulge means sure annihilation, my tormentor, I do not answer!

My adversary rallies one last time, lashing in with caustic scorn
Battering at my embittered past, my crumbling fragile walls
Hammers at my vacillating future, slamming reluctant nails
This nemesis, haunting part of me, the part of ceaseless fails
I hold back the goading, rancid tide, from myself, I will not fall!
I raise my hands to greet the skies, the tide recedes, and I stand tall!

In Olive Groves
Kate Cameron

In olive groves
Peacocks wander
golden fingers crept
over the ridge
anointing with dry heat
scattering white dust
on marble paths
ripening lemons fragrant
under the blue green mountain

113

Non-Sense
Gavin Prinsloo

Opinionated rhetoric holds the ear and feeds the fear,
Served with truth grown cold,
Voices scream and tongues demean,
And the minds of men are sold

Babble and curse feed logic in reverse,
The masses speak but do not hear,
Mouths shout and slander about,
Feeding on frenzied fear

Too many voices and too few choices,
Spins the world beyond its pace,
There is no end until all minds bend,
Peering out into the depths of space

Confusion breeds contusion,
For there is no will to understand,
That the screams of Babel
Are unable to stay a violent hand

To nature true against what we aspire to do,
Those words that we call love,
Yet the voices drown in city and town,
Hoping that we can rise above

What we believed and pain bereaved,
Lays bleeding upon the ground,
Our words are sharp and there is no harp,
To silence that dreadful sound

We fight for cause and close the doors,
We offer no love nor mercies quarter,
For in the craze and haze we set ablaze,
What was meant for son and daughter

Bury them deep for angels don't weep,
And turn away their eyes,
For the silence is loud within a blood soaked shroud,
Feeding the blatant lies

Joy Within You is Mine Too
Lana Martin

destined spaces on hillside shades
meandering grace in branches of trees
buzzing in hives of all that fades
reciting tenderly poems of bees.

like kids, we roll down the grassland
plucking field flowers' scented beauty
with no paths left behind to strand
cheering and singing in the majestic unity.

in my hands full of beats of your spirit
my happiness spreads its invisible wings
enclosed by all, within us indefinite
this joy within you, my joy also brings.

blue and purple skies stretch between us
reflecting their depths in our eyes
everything in between is just a plus
when our souls from this delight arise...

Connected Clouds
Neil Forsyth

Distant yet still connected
Those shapeless masses viewed
Above us all around us
Of rain-filled magnitudes

The distance ever changing
Life's patterns never true
Ever parting then aligning
It's what clouds and people do

Element
Imelda Zapata Garcia

Imbedded from the start
cerebral core, to heart
Crux of all that's worth
substance, since birth
Basis set in stone
marrow, to the bone
Fundamental point
engrained in every joint
Hearth of pith and pine
vat of what's divine
Sum of centerpiece
acquired upon release
Significance of Spirit
from the moment
that you hear it.
Imprinted on the Soul
what tends to make
one whole

Konrad Lorenz on Twitter
Iain Strachan

A line of little goslings
Imprint themselves on him
He's a magnet of attraction
They tail him on a whim.

Today, misinforming 'influencers'
Prowl around on X/Twitter
And bird-brained bigots imprint
Themselves on the next grifter.

Images imprint on the brain
Blazoned with meaningless memes
Thus do attention cravers
Obtain undeserved esteem.

In Times Like These
Dave Catterton Grantz

In these times, the spirit parts
Into lemon light or inky shadow,
Needing some crucible to ignite
Within a mirror that frames disdain.

Surely it must be these lemon heads.
Who absconded with security,
Who encoded artificial worlds,
Where creed has been upbraided,

Where corporations rule commerce,
Where God himself is sold away,
Where propagandists proctor and gamble
To raise their terms of endearment.

For in lemon light bask the woke,
Acquiescing to this weirding realm.
Where mirrors give birth to vipers,
Spewing bile, sustaining guile.

In times like these we can lose ourselves,
While enduring truths go to mush,
And AI Jesuses mount their sermons
On billboards and in gaudy magazines,

Along with their eleventh commandment,
"Thou shalt not show compassion
To the least of these, thy brethren."
In times like these, even hope
Goes flopping on the boards.

Waiting in the Wings
Ryan Morgan

There's a hum in the silence.
A buzzing, building surge.
It drums with impatience,
A flooding, thrilling urge
Beginning as a pinpoint of vibration,
Its noise enfolded in the hush;
A ringing, anointed manifestation
That promises to explode in a rush.

The spring wound ready
Just at the juncture of release,
Straining at its bounds, an energy
To puncture the body's peace.
A gathering of anticipation.
Breath baited, yet racing.
Quivering with internal friction.
Dreadfully elated, spirit blazing.
A focus of energy
Spearing light into the soul,
Its locus of synergy
A searing, bright coal.
The recoil between each heart's thud
Pulls more vitality into the core.
I boil as if starlight is in my blood,
A roar of electricity between the jaws.

Expectation's generation,
Energizing. Intensifying.
Imagination's acceleration,
Mesmerizing. Terrifying.
Hurtling, driving, writhing,
Humming, thrumming,
Circling, spiralling, diving,
Strumming, drumming,
Prickling, sickening,
Vibrating, dilating,
Trickling, quickening,
Excruciating waiting.....

waitingwaitingwaitingwaiting

Grinding, clenching,
Gritting, bracing,
Winding, tensing,
Sitting, pacing.....

waitingwaitingwaitingwaiting

Revising, forgetting, sweating, stressing,
Cussing, praying, blaspheming,
Improvising, regretting, wetting, messing,
Fussing, surveying, dreaming,

waitingwaitingwaitingwaiting

Crying, smiling,
Scowling, joking, choking,
Tiring, whiling,
Growling, hoping, croaking....

waitingwaitingwaitingwaiting

It's time.
A blooming vacuum of silence.
I climb
Onto the looming gloom of the dais.

I take my spot.
Earth myself to the stage.
A lightning rod
In a Faraday cage.

The silence, again.
A mute lull of torment.
The music begins.
Now's the truthful moment.

Instantaneous Angels

Peter Rivers

I wanna take you down, savage thorns,
locked crown of renown
Digging deeper bloodletting my frown,
lifted up every adjective, verb, or noun
The pressure to lead just keeps making me bleed,
drowning tide waiting to recede
Crashing with uncommon speed,
hearing from high: "You shall not proceed!"

How come something that sparkles and shines bright
just doesn't feel right?
It smothers me slow, like being inside the hourglass,
trapped unable to fight
One question, how did I get this label,
permission to sit at your table?
Did you get fooled seeing me as a rock,
somehow showing signs of unstable?

I took a shot, thought I was someone worth more,
then collapsed to the floor
It tastes like savage defeat, that door swift slammed
I didn't expect before
Off you went just one with the mist,
one thing's for sure, you're heart murmur missed
Shallow beats now, like beat from a street fight,
slipping away into the fade of night

It's so strange the life as an angel, answering prayers
Often confused like what I do is the man upstairs
I am now the sprinkles of far off whispers
helping you find your shine
Just a warmth coming over you,
blanketing breath truly divine

I shouldn't be sad I lived and never got it right,
maybe my job was to shine as the light
I could be twisted, disfigured by anger and spite,

with shadows so midnight bright
Trials of my tribulations,
inner conversations about frustrations
I have...... to take a deep breath,
and just step away
Never quit, don't surrender this way
What do you have to say,
maybe it will make me stay......

Defying Ambiguities
Scot A. Buffington

A beam once shined alone for me
doomed to glow one sacred hour
unreachable infinity
fleeting wick of candlepower.

Held by the weaker turns of fate
when woebegones a stasis made
life lived too early or too late
whatever lesser gods forbade.

To let that light shine brightly still
while absent from a distance sees
a dancing ghost, a freer will
a brighter star by vast degrees.

Though waxing melancholy spark
for any opportunities
for life alive while lit or dark
defying ambiguities.

The Violet Sheet

D. A. Simpson

The violet sheet
arching across the firmament
In the stillness
pervading the silent hour before a dawning day
Bore strands of ghostly white and pale gold

Timorous shades evoking the hesitation
hovering beyond the deserted horizon

That clung to the heavens
like breath on a cold day
Issued by a rising sun
one nascent morn

Invisible for now
beneath the line of indigo

Describing an infinite horizon
circling the seen world
Hemming the canopy
'tween this mortal realm
and the infinite dominions

Eleni

Kate Cameron

On the veranda
she swung her hair
shining in the evening air

on the far hills the peacocks cried
amid molten grasses as they dried

chicory shone in starry blue
violet skies, rarest hue.

idioms and idiots

(a dog and pony show)
Chuck Porretto

on your mark, get set, and go
dog eat dog and pony show
wag the tail, a tale of woe
choose the devil that you know
pins and needles, needles and pins
hell freeze over, the fun begins
someone loses, someone wins
hate the sinner, love the sin

that's the way the cookie crumbles
this ain't beanbag, rough and tumble
keeping score until you fumble
listen to the geezer mumble
fill the till, and fill the trough
all hands on deck, all bets are off
turn your head, now give a cough
skip the booth, but always scoff

in for penny, in for pound
pinch a penny for glory and crown
cross your bridge, then burn it down
does not matter if she drowned
off his rocker, off the hook
off the cuff, and off the books
by fits and starts, by hook and crook
look at all that loot he took

make a bundle, make a joke
laugh about the simple folk
take the fifth, and take a toke
smoke and mirrors, smoke some coke
have connections, have your way
take a seat, and take the pay
fugetabout it, what ya say
the press will make it go away

justice blind, the jury out
half will cry, and half will shout
'twas in the bag, without a doubt
the polling promised me a rout
have a heart or have a fit
take a hike or take a hit
loosen up a little bit
you know he's never gonna quit

always one in every crowd
crying out and crying loud
stop the presses, not allowed
a fall will follow being proud
a bright new rising star is born
but every rose now has a thorn
every well-known phrase is worn
and every single sheep is shorn

no prevention, a pound of cure
a pound of flesh, the soup du jour
keep it simple, keep it pure
talking points for your brochure
the truth, they say, will set you free
so pick and choose, and choose to see
hold your nose, you hold the key
take a stand, or take a knee

troubled waters, troubled times
misdemeanors, higher crimes
drop a bundle, drop a dime
cuts right through the greasy slime
a slippery eel, a slippery slope
slippery as a bar of soap
out of gas, and out of rope
just how many did he grope

we're out of time, we're out of luck
so pass the hat and pass the buck
this horse is lame, as is the duck
now watch them wrestle in the muck

so take a number, take a seat
feel the thunder, feel the heat
trick the devil, trick or treat
did you read his latest tweet

abandon hope, abandon ship
get a clue, and get a grip
let 'em fly, and let 'em rip
that one there, she used to strip
some will whine, and some will crow
watch the cocky pundits blow
a dog eat dog and pony show
now on your mark, get set, and go

A Celestial Dancer

Emile Pinet

The light;
a celestial dancer,
pirouettes;
bending and refracting,
at the crossroads
of fantasy and reality.

Weaver
of constellations,
you summon dawn's blush,
where miracles bloom
and darkness departs
at your behest;
yielding to your will.

Balancing Act
Archie Papa

Random thoughts and tangled plans
innocence shrinks and greed expands
a routine conflict and temporary love
kept hell below and heaven above

Life and death, hearts and minds
a spirit alive and the likeness it finds
time and destiny, ideas and dreams
whispered wisdom and silence screams

my forever roar for psychedelic celestials
Matt Elmore

beyond second sight transcending sound
for more of a feel about all that's abound
when slippery images take shapes of my apes
flowers in the sky reflecting interstellar lakes
as spirits arise buried now aware in the ground
with newfound eyes on what they have found

on bouncing burning butterflies of light
spreading wings we spotted allotted for sight
performing pirouettes automatic in static
enlarged charges atmospheric and electromatic
with hope on a string dancing high as a kite
star bound wishing on whatever delight I might

born for kicks fixed into this motherly core
within a perverse universe inside the outdoor
an unnatural phenomenon linked to divine joy
set about by psychedelic celestials annoyed
allowing me a blink upon their distant shore
that I may find my voice to forever *roar*!

Into the Maelstrom
Terry Bridges

I float in the light of deepening night
The blackness surrounds without any sound
Internally numb I let comfort come
I swallow whole the densest black hole
Singularity concentrated gravity
Crushes my brain I'm through the pain
Never despair there's life everywhere
Push on through each storm a new day is born
Onward travellers poetic warriors
I speak only truth desire and loss both
The universe waits the heavenly gates
Victory over fear look see and hear

Everyone Leaves
Brandon Adam Haven

Everyone leaves me to my wondrous dreams.
I'm left to paint and portrait them alone.
Then broken, I sway deeply into a bleak warning,
With fire in my eyes, yet lonely and mourning.

Chiselling away remnants of what remain,
Until I am free to escape and gleam away.
My soul flared until it can love among,
And burn the filth from my fleshly tongue.

In a sudden thought, I bathed within lost infant dreams,
And became entwined in them, deeply searching for me.
I searched and searched, and where I was finally found,
Is within a world that no longer exists, only death is bound.

Portalis

Fia Aella

Bold the timber blockade,
densely ghastly to the eye,
carved riveting trenches,
deepest pores sparing not a thing.
By a single orb of rusted ore decorated,
hinged by perishing pewter,
stern in silent tone unwavering,
dutifully fulfilling an only purpose.
Cannot I but help to wonder,
for behind such grandiose hideousness,
of what could possibly lay in wait,
requiring such hefty defence.
Materials of worth,
or materialised hopes and dreams,
to swing open freely before I,
hope does impedingly beam.
Alas! Not a quiver.
Whence and if key to be found,
sure it is to be frangible,
by the weathering of time.
Yet compelled to return a better day,
to find such another way,
the portal guarding mystery to force,
as could set I finally on merry course.
Bewildered alight with burning desire,
a want to press forward with internal fire,
long awaiting glorious transformation,
freed vow I be of such suffocation.
Impatiently now I must retreat,
by no means meaning an admit to defeat,
stay strong my friend for shall be soon,
through your frame I shall step,
no longer I nor you strewn.

Reaching
Nadia Martelli

Was it M.L.K. who first told us all
That he had a dream?
That showed me the way, a burst of hope, a call
To Freedom, to shed my screams?
I dream only for peace of mind,
Any ambition abated with age,
To not feel lonely, to be released from binds
Into Redemption, far from hatred and rage.

This, I have chased all my years,
Even time I thought I'd wasted,
For Bliss to come, encasing all my fears
And crimes I fought—now replaced
With a serenity that only love can find,
And wisdom, purity, finally whole;
So, let Serendipity hold me, make me unblind,
Not victim anymore—see, I'm reaching my goal…

Stages
R. David Fletcher

We were pretentious,
For what is youth for?
Creating stories for our crazy lives,
Imagining futures that rocked and roared.
We were sententious,
For what is mid-life for?
Inventing pasts for our searching selves,
That gleamed and shone to our very core.
We were sagacious,
For what is old age for?
Philosophy lines and comradery times,
Ever closer to eternity's door.

Life Sentence
Terry Bridges

I am an anonymity of pain
In the first circle of hell again
My friends flock like starlings
Try to help...the inmate darlings
Murmuring my occult name
I wallow in ecstatic shame

The planets slow and align
Occurrences forecast a sign
I taste only cold ashes
As my memory crashes
Icy fragments fall to earth
Awaiting a virgin rebirth

Thoughts shudder...suddenly stop
Arrested by pestilent cops
Is there an end to judgement
Trials and self-entombment?
I squirm in my cell and sweat
The agony not over yet

I venture outside mind's limits
As my sick insides plummet
No longer quietly penitent
But crazy with enragement
This is the saving hope
To escape the hangman's rope

34 Kisses
Lana Martin

thirty fourth kiss
resting on my lips
after sixteen pages
my heart engages

in the lethargic flight
beautiful and bright
within visions of your paradise
twenty first was a surprise
on page thirteen
when I was a teen
with no one around
to our faith bound
twenty one kisses
my soul misses
the land of free
under a family tree
where river flows
while bloody wind blows
thirty four break ups
in broken tea cups
tea made of petals of roses
delivered in small doses
to our childhood end
sinking into the sand
of twenty one beaches
where life teaches
lessons not learned in school
meant only to fool...
to uprise thirty four hopes
for my soul with yours elopes
leaving forty kisses for later
tipping an invisible waiter
in a cafe where they sell pain
and board children with a crane
transporting reasons
distorting seasons
for thirty fourth kiss
resting on your lips
when we were forgotten
in the fields of cotton...

Broken-Hearted Sunsets

Emile Pinet

Death came for you on a midsummer's eve,
and there was nothing I could do but grieve.
As a dying sun sets.

The air smelled of roses starting to bud,
and trickling tears soon morphed into a flood.
As lonely as it gets.

The fabric of life began to un-weave;
your death was hard to accept or believe.
Chills morphed into the sweats.

I haven't come to grips with the pain I feel,
for I want to believe this isn't real.
There are no safety nets.

Slipping into dreams you secretly haunt,
you are still the only lover I want.
My heart has no regrets.

Without you, a scarlet sunset seems gaunt,
a color nature continues to flaunt.
Broken-hearted sunsets.

Ladder to my Light

Peter Rivers

These clouds drip with honey for my eyes
A taste so gentle sweet on pillows I wait
For your vibrant kiss, is a day I can't miss
Wrap me up in the blanket of your sky
Melt me into your embrace
Take me away to your secret galaxy of stars.

The Origin
Michael Balner

I wish to reach out, touch the stars
I want to feel my fingers burn
The searing flame of endless love
One way trip only, no return

I want to fly and catch the wind
Singing atop of an old Lind tree
Then, I shall sing his song with him
Watch the leaves fall, and disappear

I need to scream and lose my mind
Float on a red wood timber raft
To where wild Nile once took my breath
And reminded me how weak I am

But when the sorrow floods my eyes
I will do nothing, I will not hide
I shall run through the fields of poppy
Into a dawn that leaves me blind

Yes, I shall tell you who I am
But first, let me walk the whole dark path
All the way back, to from whence I came
The origin of a broken heart

The Eyes of the Bridge that Sleeps
Donna Smith

Take a trip underneath its arches,
Through the eyes of the bridge that sleeps.
Float down amongst its waters,
That meanders far and deep.

Sail within its vision,
Explore all that's captured in its dreams.
Traverse in the sights it cannot take,
As you sail amongst its streams.

Behold the wonders that it holds,
That it conjures in its mind.
As you take a stroll along its path,
As it weaves and intertwines.

Experience all that it may not,
Down the paths that flow and sweep.
Take a trip underneath its arches,
Through the eyes of the bridge that sleeps.

Physics
Jessica Ferreira Coury Magalhães

It is the old heart
Bending over
Toward the time
That spills broken dreams
All over the ground.
It is the spilled time
Breaking
All over the heart
That bends old dreams
Toward the ground.

Whispers of Yesterday, Echoes of Life
Lorna McLaren

The house creaks and groans, lets out a sigh,
dust motes on the air dance gaily by,
moonbeams cast shadows on empty walls
as whispers of yesterday creep round the halls.
My childhood home, now broken and spent,
as an ongoing memory, I often frequent,
I'll sit by the window brushing my hair,
a reflection of life that is no longer there.
Nobody hears me as I silently weep,
for what was once was I can no longer keep,
while the world carries on oblivious to my plight,
no longer in focus, no longer in sight.
Forgotten to all, I have ceased to exist,
yet in death as in life there is often a twist
as I hold the last card of the hand I've been dealt
so my presence around will forever be felt.
To the ones who betrayed me, you will feel my scorn
as each night, in your sleep, a new nightmare is born,
to all others that have shown me a kindness in life
I will bring you comfort in your times of strife.
Though I wander in time, alone and bereft,
knowing of my life, in your world, nothing's left,
the essence of all that I used to be
will echo in the beyond of eternity.

Epitaph
Trude Foster

Let gentle rain fall softly as she sleeps
let tumbled grass grow long,
and wildflowers be her counterpane
let twining strands of ivy cover up her name
let her rest in peace

Autumn Breezes
Emile Pinet

September skies show signs of Fall
As geese trumpet their honking call.
But before rivers start to freeze,
Autumn breezes strip bare the trees.

October dons colors of gold,
Orange, and red, inked by the cold.
And as the hoarfrost spreads with ease,
Autumn breezes strip bare the trees.

November's clouds turn somber grey,
As nights grow cooler every day.
And though this season tries to please,
Autumn breezes strip bare the trees.

Chrysanthemums, the last to go,
Hold their blooms until the first snow.
Yet, their beauty is just a tease,
Autumn breezes strip bare the trees.

The Return
Gavin Prinsloo

The years deceased and hope released,
if only for a while,
A tender touch that meant so much,
with every thoughtful smile

You gave you took and my heart shook,
to hear that you had died,
When I was small and you were tall,
a gentle breast when confusion cried

I cannot atone for all your years alone,

as I strode back into my past,
Young and in pain my fury vain,
how could I know it could not last?

There was love I know that you would show,
although a stranger to your womb,
Today I have no voice, nor a choice
as you rest within your tomb

I fought I ran and now I can, understand
what the years have taught,
No one stands alone nor can I condone,
the pain that I have brought

The pain I caused by closing doors,
is a thing that I well know,
Now that I am old and the anger cold,
I have to let you go

Regrets that burn as emotions churn,
I will have to put away,
The past is past and not meant to last,
it belongs with yesterday

I find peace in your sweet release,
and I know that you have found rest,
Thank you from your prodigal son,
of my past you were the best

Love released when life is ceased,
a lesson I have learned,
You gave to me forgiveness free,
upon my heart your name was burnt

This is not their Time

Hahona Scribe

Mnemonic pain reverberates
crescendo unrelenting
cutting swathes
loved ones departing
This is not your time
all that's left...
are these pictures I paint of you
but the pastels turn
obsidian black
& my easel runs dry

Callous life
so young & vibrant
I dream of you
eyes shut fast
I try to live in this unknown space
feeble heart tallies not
I cannot reach you behind the veils
& memories begin to fade

Within my wanton heart
I cling to ghosts
in the dawn
in the midnight
in the twilight
& every moment in-between
I am haunted

Why must I be strong
when tears well
& I drown
in empty refrain
yet I know we shall meet again
& I too shall ascend..
the stairway to heaven
I just hope to make it in time

Dance of the Bubbles

Aaron Blackie

Dance with me, when desires
For dancing,
Bopped up like bubbles
Out of the depths
Of the rivers of wonders...

Dance with me,
Oh, steps in limbo,...
Before the famished roads—
The riding on potholes like
Undulating waves, whirling in circles
Of rumbling suspense...

Of a truth,
We danced in cyclical wonders—
Music played with muted tonality,
And noises unheard of,
Are rhythms out of scattered strings
Of hollow-eyed politics...

We planted green seeds,
And reaped yellow leaves
For staple meals, to nourish
Our recycled muscles for the
Shadowy strands,
Snarled in staled dance steps
Of yesterday, for today's
Festival of camouflage in despondency.

We measured how far we have gone—
Digging deeper the deep wells;
Measuring for
The sharp stones,
Bedded in the end-vision
Waters of promised...
But we are trapped in the red muddy Sands,
dabbled in the mingled
Waters of impurities....

Let my feet rock in the resilient dance Steps of solitude...
Whirl me, whirl me away, away from
These stagnated regions,
Submerged in darkening circles
Of puzzledom norms...

Yearning to Run
Linda Adelia Powers

The seas of the open fields are calling
I yearn to set my sails and run to my utmost
Until fulfilled I feel myself sweetly falling
The seas of the open fields are calling
Come rest in a peace finally enthralling
Leave all your worries, old fading ghosts
The seas of the open fields are calling
I yearn to set my sails and run to my utmost

Each One
Valerie Dohren

Each one gives, each one takes
Sometimes loves, then forsakes

Each one wins, each one fails
Weighs the cost, tips the scales

Each to come, each to go
Rising high, sinking low

Each one came, each one left
Hearts to bind, hearts bereft

Each one laughs, each one cries
Each one lives, each one dies

Grandpa, Draft me up!

Peter Rivers

I lick the savage steel so greasy slick
I dove to the ground lightening quick

These bombs blast, vibrations rattle my bones
Sarge says "Man up, grow a pair of stones"
I hear your voice haunt these pages like fading memory
The Texan, one of a kind friend,
our gentle giant named Gregory.
Now just a smoking pair of boots,
three seconds ago he was just there…..

Grandpa, grandpa, I'm in the hedge rows with you
I just want to help you, what do I do?
Keeping my head down was already something I knew
I'm in awe of your bravery, the caution you threw

Your manoeuvres in France, a counter
offensive to halt the enemy advance.
Day after day just pelted with rain
24/7 soggy and soaked, inches from insane
How did you have time to keep such detailed notes?
Seven lieutenants here, one dies off,
Poof, a new one promotes

Wow 38 days in a row with wet socks
Skin peels, leaving sores, while your foot rots
This is worse than prison, they get two hots and a cot.
I get half stale on spoiled rations, and hot they are not!

Oh, the wine baby, the wine!
This French stuff is so divine
Three days ago, we were at this château,
you know, stocked to the nines nothing but wine!
You ever been that kinda drunk
you can't walk or talk in a straight line?

Seriously two and three days later,

my brain is still not fine....

The ringing, the ringing,
someone answer that phone ringing......
That's not ringing, it's whistling,
death is calling, men crying, murderous singing..
All night long, bang and clash, then blinding flash
Singing, singing, haunting ringing, hours later,
heartache the grim reaper is bringing..

Lounging in the Grass
Taliesin D. Green

My soul sits cross-legged
cross-legged: firm on grass.
Grass and sky wedded
wedded as sand-glass.
Sand-glass eternal, yet...

Yet my soul sits weighty,
heavy, tired and wrecked.
Wrecked by the nth degree:
degree chaos unchecked.
Unchecked and forgotten as...

As my soul holds to green earth
earth that sings in blades of grass
grass as shifting as self-worth
self-worth that sometimes... lies scorched.

Scorched by reality's raw flames:
flames lick at the creases of hope
hope that undulates whilst it claims
claims to remain, claims to help soul cope.

Cope: a monosyllable that slides,
slides as winds and gales buffet it.
It holds, tenacious: buffeting tides
with clenched jaw. Here. Where my soul remains.

Ashes of Dawn

Peter Rimmer

Introspection
Folds me in its wake
Winter brings a sense
Of slumber
Melancholy
Dreaming time
Time folds in on itself.

Silence hangs its shroud
Over a sea of calm
Hangover equilibrium
Quiet panacea
A few song birds
A passing car
Break the calm.

Winter has cast its charm
Silence the sound
Of Winters balm
Cool air blankets
A quiescent world
Awaits the return of the sun
In the ashes of dawn.

Poets like You

Natasha Browne

Rapping,
Tapping,
Never napping,
Dancing along,
To a soundtrack,
Moving forward,
Never back,
On the right track,
Write this as I walk,

Hearing others talk,
You step up,
I step up too,
The world is lit up,
With poets like you.

I Yearn
Aoife Cunningham

By a fickle string,
I function
A fable of persistence.
Ingesting a deficit,
Enough units to reduce
the clamour of scarcity
to a gentle hum.
Yet the murmur of need
continues to bleat
Like a warning drum
I yearn.

Second Look
Richard Lambton

Second look
At first impressions
Entering the excesses
Of past transgressions;
It's all in the eye,
Or so they say,
Unable to speak,
Try as they may;
Last looks are everlasting
When what seems right
Too often feels wrong.

Azure Plume
Imelda Zapata Garcia

Wrapped in threads, woven by desire
Listens to Cicadas, singing to the Moon
Swaying to nostalgia, sits by the fire
At home, holds centuries of swoon

Creaking floor boards hum
Threats of deluge, spark with thunder
Echoing the heavens drum
Fills a night in glowing wonder

Kodachromatic celluloid on display
Strokes of genius on the walls
Ten foot ceilings mark array
Warmth of breath throughout its halls

Here she basks, in bequeathed glow
Harbors radiant, celestial gleam
Soaks in truth, she's come to know
Sips on life's elixir in each dream
This plume of turquoise bard
Treasure held within her chest
Promises to lift up guard
Share the tales, perceived at best

Turn and Toss
Steve Wheeler

I toss and turn I turn and toss
And that's how sleeping hours are lost
Insomnia affords no gloss
I toss and turn, and turn and toss

Poet Girl
Jamie Willis

I spent some time with Yeats today
And his nine and fifty swans
He soothes me in iambic
Til my agitation's gone.

I pressed the needle through the fabric
Of the right side of my dress
Drawing edges flush together
While the thread work does the rest.
It seems to me a mystery,
My frayed and weary mind
Until I stitch myself together
With the words I need to write.

A click or quill or clarion call
A mark on page, a dawning fall
The moment I when "see" it be—
Narration's smithing work for me.

Fantasia light, unborn dark
Converge in hidden story arc
Where what's unseen and what will be
Transpires in note and verse and scheme.
Mercurial looking glass concedes
The heart of man—or girl—to see.

I write to calm the storms.
I storm to fuel my write
I symbiose my soul
Within the nodes of day and night
A character of characters
An etching, scribbled stone
A meter makes my rhymed escape
Rhetoric's path to home.

In the Light of
a Hallowed Sun

Eric Aguilar

In the light of a hallowed sun,
paths have come to meet.
Heat signatures rise to the
distance of horizon's streets.
Oh, to hold a perspective, poised
by your opinion; positive, and true.
In the light of a hallowed sun is
the life of love to approach through.
For, by the cold winters of grief,
sunken shipwrecks abased in unrest.
The singing of unfound treasures
sonnet with psalm to take the breath.
A wanted calm, a peaceful token
an unspoken gesture, rekindled, kind.
In the light of a hallowed sun,
a brazen gate awaits to find.
In steps of stone unmeasured,
a heavenly script depicts the signs.
As the winds blow within moments,
in its sight, I grow and know why;
in the light of a hallowed sun.

Peacock All-Star

Peter Rivers

Burn the days in moon lit fire
Drown the nights in sun lit ire

Your Luke warm level of attraction
Failed to ever garner any traction

Cast your eyes with weak desire
Deserving all that won't transpire

147

Does courage ever come, take action
Boy, you will wait forever for a reaction

I can feel your heart I steal
In the silence, a tiny squeal

You would swear we were twins
Same sweet faces filled with sins

It excites me what we might be
I'm flutter drunk, can you see?

You're calm, I am breezy
I get so cheesy mad easy

It makes me a gimp to walk with a limp
I'm tall as a shrimp and talk like a simp
Stupid wimp you can't strut like a pimp

I wrap you in my earthen song all day long
With you, I feel I belong, is that so wrong?

Scared I wonder, will you pull me under?
This wrecking thunder, brings the sunder!

Within this tidal wave floats my grave
The pain to enslave I gave, you forgave

Truly, I deserve to strangle from every angle
Goodness I mangle, a new mess to untangle

Black fades to white as day fades to night
Is it so savage to bite with no appetite?

You were always my Angel sent from heaven
Even way back when our curfew was eleven..

Overcoming
Phyllis Angella

Stuck in a mire of
Our own design
Resistance comes knocking
I turn on a dime
The direction I was going
No longer sublime
My ego takes over
I'm no longer in line

I have a resolve to
Try harder this time
I really mean it when I say
I'm all in everyday
My intentions are pure
My thoughts on the win
But tomorrow will find me
Starting
All over again

I stay on my diet from
Dawn until 2
When a forbidden nibble
Suddenly becomes two
I love to write
But not every day
On discipline I ponder
Why it falls by the way

My childlike side wants
To come out to play
Distract from my goals
Let today waste away
My mind is a war
I've got nothing to say..

My frequency is weak
Needing a tune up to speak

I cannot manifest
I'm tired of slipping sround
Into mental low rent
And walking that ground
I'm ready for change
Good Lord here it comes
I fall to my knees and
Get the job done

A Pathway
Kenneth Wheeler

A pathway overlooked
by the intense gaze of
cherry aroma and the
pink romantic charm
that reaching out into
the rapacious arms of
spring's invited warm
embrace welcoming
the innocent into this
cluster of vibrant pink
stealing the heart of
passion, is more than
one can think,
pink colour so delicate
so feminine the blossom
perfume is so sensuous
so appealing yet not fully
understood

So Many Wishes

Becky Topham

I want to climb a mountain
Ride a bike again
Feel the wind tug my hair
Watch the summer sun wane

I want to feel the lash
Of the salt wind's whip
Taste its flavour
Upon my cracked lips

I want to lay in the fields
With the butterflies
Where the oak trees stretch
Into crayon blue skies

I want to dip my toes
Into the bubbling surf
I want to see so much
Of this beautiful earth

I want to go back
In tempestuous time
To when I was yours
And you were mine

But here are my boys
And there are my friends
Unless they are lost to me
This life never ends

And so—when I come to you
I wish to be grey and old
Embellished with stories…
Which have yet to be told

Aries Man, Part Two

Jamie Willis

Downright Ozymandiacal,
The pride before the fall
You said that you were solid gold
You said that you were strong
But the tinny tone of trumpeting...
You're just alloy after all.

I gazed into my horoscope
A wishing well, a crystal ball
But crazy eights and parlor tricks
The smoke and mirrors of bait and switch
Your empty hat, my quiet cringe
That I had hoped in you at all.

'No strings attached'—
No, just a noose
I'm struggling to cut it loose
My lips are blue
My eyes see stars
Not the kind you wish upon
The kind you see when air is gone.

Your cymbal rage
Symbolic cage
I'm trapped inside your endless roar
But sir, you underestimate
My phoenix rise through screeching gate
Where you can't hurt me anymore.

Crystal Clarity

Emile Pinet

Her presence casts an aura,
independent of sunlight;
like the glow of an angel.

Passion and desire unite,
in a symphony of hope;
orchestrated by my heart.

She is a delicate breeze,
caressing all my senses;
like the first flower of Spring.

Reflected through a teardrop,
her beauty is surreal;
in its crystal clarity.

Anticipation pumps my
pounding heart on her approach;
yet she doesn't acknowledge me.

And though my heart is breaking,
she continues to walk by;
as though I wasn't even there.

Elder Tree

Steve Wheeler

Nothing is ever all it seems to be
The rise is subtler than a hidden fee
Oh, come down from that Elder tree
There's something better here to see

A Moment
Michael Hislop

In this Moment
I can hear the stars
They are calling calling
Saying my name
The air around Me
Is dancing swirling
Carrying Me adrift
On the winds I hear Them
Come along Human
You are of the Beginning
A Moment without end

In Blank Seasons Cloaked
Brandon Adam Haven

Deep within the mind's sullen glower,
Burnt into the worn ember of ire.
The sea of the soul forever a flower,
Blanketed by the eyes of molten fire.

My words so baffling and belittled,
Pointing deep to a pale direction.
Whilst carrying a meaningless quibble,
Neath the hearth of an empty affection.

Her soft fire cannot be stoked,
Nor frozen by my timid breath.
For her veil is found in blank seasons cloaked
That unravels after cold blossoming death.

Subdued
Peter Rimmer

Thin light
Bleeds from a Constable painting sky
Brooding bruised clouds clotted
A foil to restrict sun-lights domain.

Cool air bathes a sulking landscape
Solstice time is near upon us
Where the wheel turns a slow circle
Idly rolling out the hours
Admitting a sun that smiles.

This one is shy and distant
It turns me in on myself
I retreat
Feeling empty
I've become a shadow
That needs the sun.

Black Roses
Fouzia Sheikh

You only bring me black roses
They crumble in the dust
But not under your spell.
It's a flower of darkness
Somewhere between love and hurt,
Betrayal got me here,
Only love can get me out.
You only bring me black roses
Darkness is relief,
ignorance is the cure,
but no amount of sleep.
Everything just flies on by
You only bring me black roses.

Persephone
Jenni Nichols

A goddess
in an amethyst gown,
drifts through the creases
of my dreams.
Proliferating blessings and bouquets,
she heralds the spring,
with kaleidoscopic sunbeams.

She walks
the bridge of rainbows,
as lost wings float
on invisible threads.
Suspended within this illusion,
her vibrance banishes
winter's dark dreads.

Tamburlaine
Tom Cleary

Behold before me realms of riches vast
while nodding, fearful, conquered baubled men
as holding now, disdained, their treasured past
I seek to subjugate them, pigs in pens.
Their principled ideals serve me naught
and warriors are source of love, not friends.
War is always present, fortunes bought
in victory exultant for fate's ends.
To grovel and, in pity, hope for best
sustains me not. With everlasting scorn
a sharpened spear impaled within such chest
would stop such heart of mercy now forlorn.

With ever tightening grip upon his throne
treachery nonetheless was deeply sown.

Fog the Mirror
Rafik Romdhani

I love facing the door even if it's closed
A closed door in front of you is better,
much better than no door at all.
At least you could shake hands
with the door knob before
you turn fast to yourself,
to the inward garden

I love the mirror, this murder of motion,
of action, of reaction, and of words.
This living dead we visit and revisit
every morn to make sure we are
still who we think we are,
stands like another door
into ourselves.

I love writing poems out of immobile things
but I don't want any poem of them to wait
till dawn to fly to the kingdom of minds.
I love to see my poetry fog the mirror,
open the dusty door,
and just be.

Black and White
Diana Kouprina

I prefer the black and white,
Over color any day.
As, I reside within the depth of grey.
I find, color is too blinding,
To see the essence of the way.

let them

Ayub Babikir

I would like to be still
like an ancient night or
a Phoenix egg hatching
in the eye of a storm.

but I am not that;

I am merely the shell
of that egg, shivering
at the edges of a quiet miracle.

I wish I could keep
my thoughts
by my side,
my feelings tucked to me
like wings,
but I cannot;

the news of the bombing
of a hut
in a place I heard of just now
bites my heart,
the wails of a random child
on the bus, that gets me too,
that limping dog by the road
that old beggar, that long-dead aunt and how
she sighed that evening when I
was seven
and in her voice I heard the universe
break a bit.

they all have me
my eyes my bones and
memories,
all of me, and leave me defenceless
wishing I can be like the walls
of an ancient mosque
or the scars on a time-worn face,

but I can't be any of those
only wish I could

and wishing is all I could do,
so I do it
breathe it
and live it, as the bombings
take me,
as the sick dogs and suffering children,
as the old beggars reach
for my heart, and the scars
of strangers hold my bones
in embrace,

and all I could do
is let them.

Dash
Aoife Cunningham

Life is a slow stroll of simple steps
taken over years to come.
But I seem to have taken a short cut.
Cut the distance in half.
Turned a marathon to a sprint.
Flustered feet fleeing distance.
Forgetting,
the journey is a medal, not a stretch.
Forgetting
A finish line is just that.
A finish.

One Star at a Time

Martin Gedge

To have you deep inside this heart
to follow as I go
As much in love and just enough
that you should always know
This sweet embrace of heavens grace
To fill a dreamers eyes
Behold the night as skies ignite
To light like fire flies
And through the air of comfort care
In drift of summer breeze
Each moment spur so true and pure
To spur this passion tease
A soothing touch to wrap as such
To clutch onto a thought
I stand alone each field I roam
To own what I have not
And feel of skin to take me in
To win what I deserve
That plays a tune to shoot the moon
To bloom on every nerve
So wish I may or wish I might
Each night to see you shine
No matter far or close you are
One star to make you mine…

Words are Enough

Archie Papa

The words are enough
images might bring suit
so make them articulate
and make them acute
mix them with tenacity
send 'em down the chute
to the soil of remembrance
where memories take root

The words are enough
the image isn't yours
finding those excited
and not who it bores
mix them with honesty
truth opens the doors
give them the love
no kind soul ignores

The words are enough
the image is a crutch
it's not the peacekeeper
you needed so much
let fire in the engine
let fear off the clutch
the words of emotion
and the souls they touch

With Wings that Fly
William Fields

as I dwell in the midst of hot Summer's plains
sculpting tainted remains of visions from a dream,
I weep...
yet I weep with tears of alacrity
which dampens scorching roads to prosperity
and with my head held to the sky
no said conquest can deny
awaited kinship there to be
and I will go...
oh, how I will go...
with wings that fly.

Apollo Sleeps
Valerie Dohren

The sable sky devours the dying sun
Apollo sleeps, thus silent be his lyre,
So I shall sleep, for now the day is done
And shadows fall beneath the fading fire

As Luna softly smiles upon the night
Apollo sleeps, with laurel wreath adorned,
And darkness takes his place to steal my sight
The closing of the day forever mourned

For blinded thus, my soul no longer sings
(Apollo sleeps, the poet's heart then stilled)
All thought has flown upon celestial wings
My heart no more to dance, no more fulfilled

Apollo sleeps, I pray that he shall wake—
My spirit, life, and soul, no more forsake

I am on Fire
Gavin Prinsloo

Crimping, curling
Dust falling, ash whirling
Sub-cutaneous words scorched by fire
Smoke pouring into the funeral pyre
Into?
That can't be right
Smoke rises, out of sight?
Smoke and heat pour back into my repose
Nothing recognizable from head to toes
Where is it going?
Is the flame all knowing?
Conflagration consumes every tiny part
Of the void I would call my heart
Listen...what's that sound?
Cracking bones explode as the flames consume
Only ash left to inhume
Look...what is that?
Is it ink that runs in a carbonised stream
Or perhaps the blood of a poets dream

The Colour of Silence
Charlene Phare

Whispered hues of snowfall
The colour of silence
As summer tries to install
There's whispered hues of snowfall
The birds quietly call
In their humbling defiance
Amid whispering hues of snowfall
Secreting colours of silence

Bus Enthusiast
Aoife Cunningham

I wish I could strap wheels to my feet
like Heelys.
Or jump on my flicker and scoot.
Cycle down cobble roads
to reach the places I need to go.
Walk for miles without test.
No volcanic activity on my heels.
No inflated feet.
Glide over drive.
No tax to count or petrol to note.
This mode of going
is great if you're brawny.
I am scrawny.
With flagging calves.
A body covered in the glue of distant wounds.

The bus stop is a distance from my cradle.
A stretch that would crumble my titanium.
A mile is painkillers.
So I am passenger bound.
Dependent on Mother's gas,
Because her daughter believes
She is too high-strung for a motor.
Too flighty for steering.

It's true.
I rely on Google to get to Tesco,
and will somehow manage to do
another wrong turn till the tills close.
No milk for my oatmeal.
The damn arrows kept getting confused.

Honestly, I am not even a safe pedestrian.
I dodge cars frequently. Lost in thought.
Counting how many yellow hats I saw.
It was 7 last Tuesday. I dodged an Audi.

I see a truck. I close my eyes.
Afraid the wheels would devour me
from the concrete.
It has never happened,
but you never know
when an engine will be hungry.

I do understand these anxieties
will be squashed through the mastery of machine.
Yet I still believe
the metal box of a bus
would feel safer
than the snug seats
of a Cooper.
Motion is in the lap of the captain.
All I have to do is wear my seatbelt.

lament #6 repugnant politician
Matt Elmore

hypocritical analytical incredulous flop
bottomless treasure, fettered in rot
steeped in viciously pernicious plots
beauty once given, now the devil has got

calm promises embalm songs in the dark
venomous vapor labors pet poisoned hearts
singing unclean angels estranged; evil in art
direct your tart dart into this partisan mark

impurely lure me, you well-dressed mess
coax pokes with a hoax; never confess
flaunt your font, clogged with but one guess
as to how abscess infects such finesse

wretched politician pleasured by pain
obscure your cure and we'll do the same

Loyal Wrong
Karin J. Hobson

In what moment did eons pass
taking to amass time,
Where lit candles on church mantels
counted seconds in a crime?

Flicker, flicker like wristwatch ticker;
Remind, remind to rewind;
The hour ever surrounding a breath
Where death is but a snuff away;

Liken to a winding staircase climb
Where step by step seals a rhyme;
Click, click, compares to tick as
Destination nears;

Does not eternity's hum strum
Forever and a day?
And, giant store-mount clocks
like Big Ben halt the walk to stay?

Why buy time in what needs be done
And, not by way of completions sum?
Do you count next breath's exhale
as inhale rounds the corner?

No, no said Autumn to Winter
The stopwatch has no pleasure;
But, come, come sundial's sun
Satisfaction is in the measure

Time is but a pendulum swung;
Man tied to a layman's pride;
Uncoil mankind's loyal wrong
And, sweet serenade the present!

Currency

Gregory Richard Barden

time …
takes no hostages
but for those let with dearest blood
if there *is* such a thing as chaos
it is in the scrambled madness
that intent, circumstance, fate, and impulse
leaves upon our plate …
we trade the futures of our youth
for the memories of age
the dearest cost—
each moment, each instant—
given without a thought of how
incredibly precious it is
how valuable its utilization …
and it's amidst that casualty that we
lose sight of the little things
the in-between happenings that become
the thread of our lives—
that gold braid that binds all we do and
think and feel and find
to our desires and achievements
and sews the seam of
existence, grace and hope …
yet …
we all have the option
(and it is a self-conscious choice)
to not accept time's tariffs—
to appreciate a moment with the
reverence it's due
and not assess our worth by accomplishment
but rather how fully we embrace the now
and the only true lasting, timeless
treasure …
love.

Yada Yada Yada, Experts Warn
Iain Strachan

Electric fans make rooms hotter, experts warn.
Yoghurt linked to cancer, experts warn.
Staring at moon lunacy, experts warn
Intermittent Fasting linked to heart disease, experts warn.
Sudoku causes Alzheimer's, experts warn.
Putin to nuke UK, experts warn.
Baked beans make greenhouse gases, experts warn.
Election debates linked to smashed TV screens, experts warn.
Plague of ants about to take over world, experts warn.
Playing Monopoly makes you a capitalist, experts warn.
Collapse of civilisation imminent, experts warn.
Average IQ about to plummet, experts warn.
No evidence exercise beneficial, experts warn.
Electric vehicles likely to explode, experts warn.
Planet Earth on collision course with Mars, experts warn.
Tabloid headlines bad for mental health, experts warn.
Experts' warnings can be wrong, experts warn

Twenty Six and Two
Archie Papa

Time is distance
truth is real
fear we imagine
love we feel

Forever has patience
never can't wait
the past has experience
the future has fate

...twenty six words and 2 stanzas (the title is the poem). While the time we capture the attention of reader is short, we should try to put a great amount of meaning in few words. Find the shortest path to remembrance.

Breakable
Steve Wheeler

We are all breakable
It's unmistakable
Our souls are takeable
There is no unbreakable

I'll Step Out Again
Roger Simpson

I'll step out again
On the route
So familiar
Hoping to catch your eye

With a ready
Self-deprecating
Smile
And an invitation

That I would probably
Stumble over
If you ever
Did look me in the eye

Ever hopeful
Ever foolish
Ever lost
To this ridiculous game
I play with myself

That you have
No idea of

Invasion
Linda Adelia Powers

Believing it improbable
In lifetimes unremarkable
We doubted as we stood in crowds
Aliens breaking through the clouds
In black lightning and sideways cyclones
Rotating triangles came searing our homes
Moaning we are done, our history finished
Vanquished we will soon perish famished
Standing on rooftops in meadows
Frozen holding hands to our mouths posed
We gasp waiting for signs of extinction
Stunned wishing for we don't know what, Intuition?
Struck by how much sense our lives made
Even with death for our ends traded
Others living on made our lives bridges
We hadn't acknowledged by degrees
How we could love our own species,
All the possibilities of humanity rhyming.
Now we are waiting for a double death
Ourselves and all others for all time
Somehow we never believed
It could be

I am a Warrior
Chiledu Ohagi

I wedge a war against my feelings
pulling down strongholds
breaking the chains of depression
My pages, my battleground
My pen, my mighty weapon
and my ink's my ammunition

I am a warrior
I strive for inner peace
I seek liberation all around.

Standing firm, I won't slumber
I'll conquer all
and emerge the victor

I am a warrior,
breaking the cedars
with nothing but my words
through the love of the art
I'll surpass
and have the last laugh

Into the Dreaming

Ryan Morgan

Through each flickering image
I quest ceaselessly,
Searching for the first dream.

Throw myself from the waking bridge,
Immersed in sleep's fluidity,
Quenching my thirst in its stream.

The riot of pictures bring slippage
Awash in the Leith's chilly
Fathoms which accursedly gleam.

But yet I still unflaggingly voyage,
Slavishly rowing fearlessly,
My mind a traversing trireme.

In this shadow-winged pilgrimage,
Subconsciously roaming sinuously,
I seek the cosmological theme.

I float on reality's sinking wreckage
Before the Gates of Horn and Ivory
As truth and falsity teem.

Even if I behold the divine visage
Frescoed on the walls of eternity
It will vanish on waking like a moonbeam.

171

The Sirens' Refrain
Steve Wheeler

The distant sirens
bring a tuneful colour
to the white noise
of incessant traffic.
They carve the air
as they wail their
solemn melodies
in undulating waves:

(Some-day
I wish
upon a star...)

But chaos reigns
at journey's end.
A destination filled
with tragedy or pain.
No rainbow awaits
at the conclusion
of the sirens' refrain.

How
Gregory Richard Barden

o how do moons deceive the dusk
one breath from gone to there ...
like tapestries with Guipure lace
stained soft with blue ... and bare?

o how should I yet mourn the day
with what blooms east-to-west ...
a vault with colored bib and stars
bright jewels to grace its breast?

o how does spindrift wend its way
to span such breadths of tide ...
its toes a-dancing brine-top breaks
while black, those depths abide?

o how can hearts not blossom bright
when children's laughs abound ...
to heal the hopeless, broken souls
through noise of sweetest sound?

o how can promise, given when
impassioned flesh thus flowers ...
hold strong against a yearn of years
those truths that change devours?

o how could she then bind me tight
those oaths she spurned herself ...
hope's garland left to gather dust
shunned with'ring 'pon her shelf?

o how can simple words compel
the coursings, deep our blood ...
or stain a page in wisdom, sage
shape statues grand, from mud?

o how can we keep children safe
from monsters 'neath their beds
when evil's face is commonplace
masked false with love instead?

and how should I find loves to fill
these holes thrust thru my heart
if that dear cost of what I've lost
has ripped these bones ... apart?

o please ... where should I start?

Grandma's Cup

Graeme Stokes

He's fallen into a dark and lonely space
His anxious nerves frazzled and cooked
He has his errant mind to chase
But can't distinguish trees from wood

His troubled past, a hard escape
The haunting tribulations stalk
He relives the pain of yesterday
His pallid features blank and gaunt

A fragile line draws his existence
His uphill struggle descends tough
But hot brew warms up his mission
For there's solace in Grandma's cup

A frail grip takes hold his sanity
His lucid moments, sparse
But there are glimpses of sweet clarity
Though the flavour never lasts

For his obsession, much conjecture
Why it's held with such devotion?
This sacred mug that interjects
To set his world in motion

He finds peace within his milky tea
She soothes his journey rough
But why she stirs him stays a mystery
It's between him and Grandma's cup

If I Don't Wake up Tomorrow
Paul Ross

If I don't wake up tomorrow, don't cry for me,
For my spirit will roam free, unbounded and wild,
In the whispering wind and the sunset's golden spree,
In the laughter of children and the songs of the mild.

I'll dance among stars, painting skies with my dreams,
And linger in memories, in every sunbeam's gleam.
Embrace the dawn with a heart full of grace,
For my journey continues in a far-off place.

Remember me not with tears, but with a smile,
As I journey beyond, mile after infinite mile.
For life is a fleeting, transient show,
And in each goodbye, a new hello.

What if Truth Wasn't True
Stephen Loch Bowie

What if truth wasn't true?
If you couldn't tell the diff what would you do?
Take each statement at its face
Every argument embrace
This is me asking you.
What if lies didn't count?
Your own version of the sermon on the mount?
Weave a narrative that suits
Button up the old jack boots
You'll succeed—I don't doubt.
In the end will we see
If I'm changing you or if you're changing me
Will we leave a bloody field
Neither one of us will yield
In the end: tragedy.

Cobweb Days
Sean D. Timms

You may cut me with your serrated eyes
Shoot me with your barbaric words
Just when you think you have me down in place
Once again I fly away

You may cover my soul with your cobwebs
As I gather the dawn in stone echoes
My song lilts on a gossamer labyrinth
Of moonlight hours

I think of us when our song
Penetrates my membranous labyrinth
We are each other's relief from
A cacophony of tone deaf sycophants
Each other's equilibrium

I fell into a drowning pit
Torn clothes my dreams attire
Full of seething anger and remorseful regrets
In my darkest nightmare
You saved me you pulled me closer
In your darkest day dream you learned
That I'll be there to save you to pull you closer
I think of you in this aquarium dream
Laying there in a crumpled heap
Your aura reminds me of flowers

Once again

Die to these Shields

Kate Cameron

Die to these shields
let us be a lover, to life, to man
pretence shatters

under a forgotten sun
we paint the picture

sometimes black as a sheet of tar
or as a soft black cat
watercolour at the edges

egrets stalk in snowy beauty
under white cherries as the creek flows
really see

Segments of life
a hit of juice or gooseberry tart
veracity bites
eat the fruit,
press me back
into an image

I run and meld like mercury
you are my mirror
I see you
even when my eyes
become stars

Coffee grounds tell me
there is a slim chance against the odds
to dance
to flare into metaphorical insolence
I sullenly walk the line

Come to me in the wild woods
under kaleidoscope of leaf shadow
on the warm earths bed

tear our manifesto
to beds for mice

to magnify until glass
catches the sun
crisply curls to nought
and silence comes unsolicited unsought

A Butterfly in Flight
Emile Pinet

Earth is a place of beauty and wonder,
hosting a slew of creatures, big and small.
But butterflies are hailed among Nature's
masterpieces as unique works of art.

Caterpillars morph into winged fairies,
through the magic of metamorphosis.
And live phantasmagorical paintings,
in all colors of the rainbow; take flight.

Splendiferous delicate filigree
intricately guilds iridescent wings.
And silver, blue, green, and crimson combine;
into abstract patches painted by light.

Taking Her art to another level,
Nature is an unparalleled artist.
And as a testament to Her talent;
a butterfly in flight is breathtaking.

Madman
Ayub Babikir

this year was a madman
walking with his hands
holding in his toes, red caskets
small as bird cages, holding flowers that,
whenever he waved to a passing bullet,
would bleed yellow.

this year
was a madman dragging
one season, painted with blue fog,
through four shades of mourning,
singing happily to old
sad tunes.

this year
was a madman planting,
by the sides of the streets, nostalgia
to the old boot
the old chain
the old fang and whip.

this year
was a madman stealing
from heaven
her book of the good and beloved
and renaming it: the dead;
all the best people I know,
the angelic
the pure as dew
the lighter than happiness
the so sweet as to be taken
for spring in clothes,
they all went out, like candle flames.

this year
was a madman with a terror
of late night phone calls
motorcycles

door knocks after dark,
a terror of quiet
empty walkways, of laughing loudly.

this year
was a madman firing,
from behind his tabby shawl,
a blast that shatters body
after body
family after family
desire after dream
after hope.

this year was 365 notes
of sorrow
of flavours of grief in rows.

this year
was a mad, mad, madman
happy in his madness.

Out of the Blue
Charlene Phare

The mirror broke years ago
Well over seven years
Since then I've been challenged
And fought against frosty fears

Times they are changing
For the better not worse
We look to the future
To eliminate the curse

Woken from the sleep walk
Into pastures new
Warmer tones appear now
In recovery from the blue

Wrath and Grace
William Fields

to what purpose might the hurricane serve
when she mangles and mauls earth's face
one might argue her origin's intent
as the wrath states methodically its case

she anchors one foot in the ocean
as the other commences on land
her readiness precedes anticipated death
and destruction on its command

her harsh indignation and desecration
of souls as she breaches the shores for smite
disseminates acts of her vile cruelty
and stokes the inhabitant's fright

some claim her dreaded nature
parades a fate not suited for this earth
yet her malice exposes a hidden cognition
which reveals an exceptional birth

enlightenment born from the etchings
of grief is exalted when brought to one's face
had not been for wrath and the wakening
conscience we'd tarry to recognize grace

Poets Poetry Block Blues

Sarah Joy Holden

Ink well is dry
I fail when I try
It makes me cry
I can't think why

I used to be prolific
Now it is pathetic
Far from being terrific
Never is it poetic

A nation expects
Yet nothing connects
Just lots of rejects
No food for critics

Even this is useless
My poetry is fruitless
No found excuses
Just totally pointless

I can't think why
It makes me cry
I fail when I try
Ink well is dry

Liberation

Kate Cameron

Are we limitless
an elegant angelus of pure emotion
the colour of absinthe
you write an eternal overture
starving I see you liberating pigments
like Chardin
simple as a Japanese sleeping mat
did you see the ripe corn beyond itself

compare an aromatic China rose with
an al fresco whiff of fresh mint

the spiritual hunter gatherers
abrasive false king
with strong box energy
sputters nervously

heartbreaking you
you are balance
I am eternally loveless, aloof
ripping beautiful pigments
in elemental transient embrace
and oh, worth liberating.

Risen
Darren Burt

When soul meets body
A vision to behold
Voice of reason
Words to be told
Come to the splendor
Rise throughout the night
Light of awakening
All will be alright
Hear the chorus
Listen for the appeal
Angels are trumpeting
Of one's life to steal
Taken from this earth
To a heaven above
Spending eternal joy
In God's almighty love

Falling
Andy Reay

Do you ever feel like you're falling
One moment safe, under bed covers
The next, you tumble backwards
Your hands grip the sheets,
and you can't breathe

Imagine if you did fall
Calm bedroom air, suddenly becoming chill
Clothing soaked with sleet, ice in your hair
Your backwards downhill journey suddenly stops,
as your clothes are caught on a branch

You look down into an endless chasm
and hear the fluttering of bats
One wing hits your face,
a hook scratching your eyelid
Blood obscuring your vision

You wonder, if the branch snaps,
will you fall to your death,
or will you wake up?

Search for the Infinite
Anita Chechi

In search of the Infinite
The mind runs
Like a deer runs
In search of water
Then the threads of attachment pull
Back to the world
Like the wind pulls
The clouds towards itself
In this internal conflict
Lightning flashes in the sky and in the mind.

Pantomime of Dreams
Janet Tai

All afternoon
Been swatting
Been chasing
Away those annoying
Blues;

Alone....
Huddled in my room
On the bed in foetal
Position
I have the four walls
For companions;

Back and forth
We converse
But it's only my voice
That resounds
Back to me
In silent weeping
I go again;

At last...
The sun has set
I'm able to welcome
The darkness
Into its core, I enter
Into oblivion
Into a pantomime
Of dreams!

Deniers

Ilya Shambat

In America and Australia there's a growing hysteria
Comparing those who see global warming threat
To the North Koreans and the Soviets.
Mr. Inhofe said scientists lied to you,
I don't subscribe to that point of view
It's such an ignorant thing to tell
I hope deniers love their kids as well.

How can I save my little girl
from the rule of Texas Oil?
We see misuses of common sense
By those the Right side of political fence
They don't care about biology
But only their false ideology
Believe me when I say to you
I hope deniers love their children too.

These people claim rationality
as they deny planetary reality
And believe to be the soul
of the nation as they practice prevarication
Freedom and wealth do not require
To burn oil or set rainforests on fire.
Mr. Limbaugh said it can't be true,
I don't subscribe to that point of view,
It's such an ignorant thing to tell
I hope deniers love their kids as well.

The facts of climatology
Are not dependent on ideology
What might save us, me, and you
Is if deniers love their children too.

Gimme a Break!
Shirley Rose

I'm gonna take an Adjournment from Allegory
A Sojourn away from Sonnet
I definitely need a Hiatus from Haiku
And get Offline from the Ode
Evacuation from an Elegy I certainly need
And Cessation from Cinquain would suit, indeed
I need a Vacation from the Villanelle
A Trip away from Triolet
Give me a much-needed
Respite from Rondel
A Break from the Ballad
Put me on Pause from the Pastoral poem
I think I deserve a Furlough from Free Verse...

I am having reluctance to rhyme
My mind is fried—my time is my time!
Everyone else is having a ball
Celebrating Summer!
See you in the Fall...

Zombie
R. David Fletcher

The quantified self,
Spectre of silicon men,
Live not their digital lives,
Observe to merely record them.
The measured self,
Evolution of biological fate,
Programmed by the market master,
Biting at the electron bait.

Polaroid
Tim Queen

I've got an old one
of her

out near the garden.
smeared orange

and red, smiling,
hanging laundry,

clothes pin in her
mouth in her

ready dress
and hat and a

poem on her
sleeve. she was

slightly out of
focus, timeless

near forgotten
but here she is valid

in the old nostalgic
summer

I can keep her
frozen here

it proves she
existed she

loved and struggled
smiled and cried

listened to
cicadas

the breathing of
the crickets

and watched the
scattering of

stars in the
Ohio night sky.

Mirage
Valerie Dohren

There are only shadows—
no substance
to an evaporating world.

Time has etched its purpose upon my soul,
eroding away all vestiges of hope,

and life has written the score
of a melancholy tune
upon my heart.

The way forward
is now obscure—

for the path is overgrown with weeds
and bracken.

Yet

looking towards the sun,
do I see a new dawn on the horizon,
a world of promise?

Through blurred eyes—
a mirage unfolds
in the distance.

Ashen Sheen
Donna Smith

Above the cobalt skies the melancholy moon plays its dark nocturne provoking the sky to switch from blue into the grey, forming a chalky ashen sheen.

The sun awaits its turn to rise, planning an ascent, it's time to shine and turn the darkness into light, throwing shades of orange and yellow beams which cast a marmalade hue onto the horizon. The season has now turned to fall with autumn shedding and throwing off its unwanted burdens.

My little eye notices this broken house on Constellation Road, there are dim small lights burning, flickering, performing the dance of the metaphors beckoning me forth to venture closer, nearer, beyond the pyre.

Going Missing
Fadi Yousef

She walks the city at night
Her feminine side under the moonlight
The insomniac stars wide awake
As the cold assimilates in alleyways
Where the homeless warm themselves
With cigarettes and nips of rum
The rats and darkness
Nipping at their heels
As the moon crosses over
The abridged sky shade by shade
And phases of sprinkles populate
The empty streets
Before a full migration of rain
Floods the metropolis
Wetting freshly delivered newspapers
With headlines about women
Going missing in the midnight shadows

The Fire that Burns

Ilya Shambat

The fire that burns in me today
Will also burn in me tomorrow
In all derangement and all sorrow
Its shadow shall the walls display.

Outside the opening of a cave
Or out of the volcanic crater
Is seen the truth of the creator
And everything that he may save.

It is in everything that's true
And also everything apparent—
The sky, illumined and transparent,
Alit in pink and white and blue—

Reflects him as though through a prism
And into multi-colored splendor
The universal truth is rendered,
Like lava bursting through the schism.

The fire that burns in me today—
A spark of all-consuming plasma—
Will percolate like a miasma
Into the place where shadows play—

Will burn the skin of all therein
And fill their noses full of poison
And make the place destroyed and noisome
Until in caves they can't remain;

But burst into the higher mind
From higher mind to higher senses
And as their spirit-form advances
They see the sun, but go not blind—

But burn through stone, through barren rock

And smash and tear and rise to passion
Shaking the earth like a concussion
And time resetting like a clock.

Water in heights; in water, heights—
In heights of mind exists life's essence
And in its gentle incandescence
At truth of universe arrives

In water, heights; and as its waves
Engulf, caress the restless kernel
Etheric merges with infernal
To cleanse the confines of the cave,

And send its members through the core—
Into the ever-waiting heaven—
And then return unto the cavern,
This to repeat forevermore.

A Life in Slow Motion

Jenni Nichols

I sit atop the blustery bluff,
and watch as the ocean
swells and undulates
towards the rocky cliff face,
anticipating each explosion,
while billions of droplets
hurl themselves
rebelliously into the air,
and frothy crowns
form tumultuous filigree
upon the deep blue breakers.

And, for all this intensity,
there is a slowness,
like watching a film panning slowly,
frame by frame...
and I give thought to the fortuity
that if I were able to view my life,

---

in this same slow motion wont.

Could I stop the heartbreak
before it happened,
or keep a loved one with me
for just a little longer?
Would I erase that time when
I made a complete fool of myself,
and relish in the joy of replaying the delicious bits,
over and over?

But, I have a sneaking suspicion,
that herein lies the reel magic
of life's silver screen.
You only get one opportunity to
take 'the shot'
to make the most of
every minute,
every breath,
every life,
every love...

To be prepared for when
the waves crash onto the shore
and send you tumbling,
head over heels,
and for when,
it's time to lay back
and relax in the warm, calm water,
with the sun on your face.

Every split second becomes a story,
each frame is a print.
There is no time to edit,
and there are no great reams of celluloid
spilling onto the cutting-room floor.

this is real...
live in this moment...
project your greatness...

Ghetto Blues

Chiledu Ohagi

I witness daily this pain
the unravelling of this world
into a dark and cruel place
a place where wishes die,
and dreams are never reality
the only reality is suffering.
Where the top cats roar so loudly
and we're humbled in tears.

A crisis filled paradise
where even the elders cry,
and the youths gnash their teeth
"Why, oh why does wealth linger?"
the smiles of children are no more,
it is wiped out by hunger.
Wars breaks forth from all sides,
and yet no peace is found

Is this hell?
Or a horrible nightmare
Good lord, wake us up right now
Our souls are weary,
we are struggling to live
whipped and battered
Our desires are crushed daily;
the only tunes we hear,
are the screams of pain everywhere
and this alert "He couldn't make it."

Breakfast with Greenfinches
Trude Foster

Breakfast at my table
on a damp warm morning
with birds in the trees
each fluttering one a note which sings,
on high and leafy hidden wings
that beat to lift in heavy air
which chained to the ground
I cannot share
their joy in endless headlong flight,
that freedom brought of skies delight
and so for now, to me it seems,
I must content myself with dreams

The Mousetrap
E. C. McCaffrey

The stage has been set for a satire
A farce on a comedy of liars
There was the fool who knew far too little
And the loon who had grown much too brittle
There was the rich man with a nasty tongue
He wore the lynchpin of a smoking gun
Watching in wings were the puppeteers
The master kings that pulled the strings and gears
Beyond the curtains of this hippodrome
A fate uncertain just like the fall of Rome
Those whispered fears by lips who have a plan
Blister the ears and strip the peace from man
The audience is gripped by silent awe
Plebeians tricked into their violent squalls
A spin of words reveals the final act
To win the herds and bring them to the trap
This wicked game, born out of filthy lust
Tell me now shame, where is your guilty blush!

Lopped
Gregory Richard Barden

I thereby pledged to leave alone
endeavors bound for ills, my own
to worship at your fleshly throne
and bow before your pleasures
their ends, quite at your leisures

oh all my prayers are met, replete
while fawning honors at your feet
ten hot-pink piggies, soft 'n' sweet
lined straight as little misses
kept clean for courtly kisses

I'm just a jester—scoundrel, true
one foolish fool for moonlite, blue
when daubed upon the husk of you
pearled garland for your bedding
to naughty knots, we're heading

yet while I worship yours, all-in
and fan our friction, skin-to-skin
you call another's name (with sin)
and perfect passion moulders
so cleaving, as it smoulders ...

this fool's head ... from his shoulders.

God Screams
Rafik Romdhani

God screams into my head,
there is a deep, deep, dark sea
of utter vileness and cruelty.
A drunk present almost dead,
away from tears, above a cloud,
watches a people forever bleeding
and painfully bathing in its blood.

Where the Final Thoughts Reside
Kevin Francis

They all passed this way
Those who raged
Those who wrote the rage
The best of us
Genius, clown, thief and tyrant
Met with the dying of the light
And in the end stared at the truth
Eye to eye at the meeting of the ways
Where the final thoughts reside

Doesn't It?
Lana Martin

doesn't it feel like rain
full of faith
spreading down your lungs
in every molecule of oxygen
another planet
doesn't it feel like another world
gliding down your skin
like words made of snow
melting in impossibilities
of yesterday's charm
of tomorrow's love
doesn't it feel like thunder
coming from your fingers
the power of togetherness
the lightning of unity
faithfully breathing out
on my lips
in my embrace...

Surrounded by Busts
Ligor Stafa

Amid inquisitive and nonchalant gazes,
You feel an abrupt sting,
A gypsum's resounding slap,
A cunning mind at play,
And meanwhile, do you choose to stand or not?
Do you stand or not, in the space
Where the Self has taken its place?
And you, entangled in the incomprehensible,
Pose the question to the comprehensible:
Why not leave autographs once more,
Don Quixote of Mancha,
Narcissus II?
Why don't they want to let you
Stay, even here, in this corner
Of the grand hall?
Why,
When there are still vacant seats?

Journey to a Dark Place
Linda Falter

I am not on the inside looking out
I am on the outside looking in

I am wrong side out
I said but did not speak
I wrote but could not write
I am listening but cannot hear
I am looking but cannot see
I am feeling but cannot be
I am not within me
I am everywhere
I am not here....
I am free

The Philosopher's Paddle
Martin Gedge

Come and take a ride with me to a place beyond the soul
Where every page will show its age in symmetry and flow
To open eyes to starry skies on wings that fly on beams
To take you through this wondrous view so beautiful it seems
A fantasy of make believe a destiny you sail
As to unfold the dreams you hold to tell each road a tale
And to embrace of love and grace this place beyond your years
To settle in this comfort grin on skin to spin your fears
That to unknown this flesh and bone and tone it will adore
Your open heart right from the start in light of so much more
And from each line this broken spine you find unto it grips
A sea of blue that answers you as true to soothe the lips
In every word you ever heard to sound absurd with tongue
Each twist of verse of prize and purse will thirst before the sun
And drawn of night an ocean flight as bright to light this room
In silent still the stars at will to shine this midnight moon
Of pearl and peace of sweet release to feast with open eyes
The more you feel it seems unreal to seal what it implies
That shall it pass for one to last and grasp the coming storm
You must be strong to just hold on to breathe and weave its form
To play the page that takes the stage as to engage the book
I'm sure you'll find what blows the mind each time you take a
look…

Future Camera
Steve Wheeler

Future camera, train your lens on me
Pull your focus, what will be will be
Let the F-stop measure my exposure
Write my refrain like Lamont Dozier
Capture my life in monochrome
Call my lawyer on the telephone
Future camera, train your lens on me
Pull your focus, what will be will be

Hidden Notes

J. Henry DeKnight

Ten thousand blades of grass
One million grains of sand
Five hundred drops of blood
dripping off my hand

The knife that cut the skin
The blade that cut the lawn
The wave that crashed the beach
To make the right things wrong

A cloud can bring down rain
to cleanse the wicked soul
Ten thousand blades of grass
to make a half man whole

One million grains of sand
That slip from glass to glass
minutes bleed through hands
as the hours pass

The knife that cut the skin
The blade that cut the lawn
The wave that crashed the beach
That makes the greatest song

rock bottom mountain

Matt Elmore

come see rock bottom mountain
it's a long way to the top
with every step a potent prayer
every failure a dangerous drop

where doubts cause many a stumble
breezes cool beaten brows
many sweats become humbled
empowered within future nows

some question why even try
so very far from home
it's so much easier down in the valley
where heights aren't so overblown

yet at the vista take heed
there's no more room to roam
whether up or down, one comes to believe
we need never struggle alone

for there is an assisted sight unseen
to an eternally flowing fountain
of wizened bursts for all who thirst
to climb rock bottom mountain

Denouement

R. David Fletcher

In the black hole of the bio machine,
In the interstices of the neuron matter,
Constellations of images beam,
On memory's screen left tattered.
Grasp identity's receding sight,
The fading ghosts in memory's bed,
Dissolve in dreams as mind takes flight,
The blankness of the walking dead.

About Wheelsong Books

Wheelsong Books is an independent poetry publishing
company based in the ocean city of Plymouth,
on the beautiful Southwest coast of England.

Established by poet Steve Wheeler in 2019,
the company aims to promote previously unheard voices
and encourage new talent in poetry. Wheelsong is also
the home of the Wheelsong Poetry anthology series,
featuring previously unpublished and emerging poets
from around the globe.

Wheelsong has more poetry publications in the pipeline!
You can read more about Wheelsong Books and its growing
stable of exciting new and emerging poets on the
Wheelsong Books website at:

wheelsong.co.uk/publications

Wheelsong publication list

2020
Ellipsis by Steve Wheeler
Inspirations by Kenneth Wheeler
Sacred (2020, Revised 2024) by Steve Wheeler
Living by Faith by Kenneth Wheeler
Urban Voices by Steve Wheeler

2021
Small Lights Burning by Steve Wheeler
My Little Eye by Steve Wheeler
Ascent (2021, Revised 2023) by Steve Wheeler
Dance of the Metaphors by Rafik Romdhani
Into the Grey by Brandon Adam Haven
RITE by Steve Wheeler
Absolutely Poetry Anthology 1 by various

2022
Absolutely Poetry Anthology 2 by various
War Child by Steve Wheeler
Hoyden's Trove by Jane Newberry
Shocks and Stares by Steve Wheeler
Autumn Shedding by Christian Ryan Pike
Cobalt Skies by Charlene Phare
Wheelsong Poetry Anthology 1 by various
Rough Roads by Rafik Romdhani

2023
Symphoniya de Toska: Book One by Marten Hoyle
Vapour of the Mind by Rafik Romdhani
Nocturne by Steve Wheeler
Symphoniya de Toska: Book Two by Marten Hoyle
Wheelsong Poetry Anthology 2 by various
Constellation Road by Matthew Elmore
Beyond the Pyre by Imelda Zapata Garcia

Symphoniya de Toska: Book Three by Marten Hoyle
Wheelsong Poetry Anthology 3 by various
This Broken House by Brandon Adam Haven

2024
All the Best (Poetry 2020-2023) by Steve Wheeler
Invisible Poets Anthology 1 by Invisible Poets
Darkness into Light by David Catterton Grantz
Wheelsong Poetry Anthology 4 by various
Marmalade Hue by Donna Marie Smith
Melancholy Moon by Gregory Richard Barden
Average Angel by Matthew Elmore
Storming Oblivion Peter Rivers
Circus of Circles by Aoife Cunningham
Wheelsong Poetry Anthology 5 by various
Stealing Fire by Tyrone M. Warren
The Infinite Now by Steve Wheeler

2025
Off the Top of My Head by Graeme Stokes
Creative Deviance by Steve Wheeler
Invisible Poets Anthology 2 by Invisible Poets
Invisible Poets Anthology 3 by Invisible Poets
Wheelsong Poetry Anthology 6 by various

The **Wheelsong Poetry Anthology** series – raising funds for Save the Children worldwide relief fund.

These and all other titles are available for purchase in paperback, and Kindle editions and some in hardcover on Amazon.com, direct from wheelsong.co.uk or by emailing the publisher at: wheelsong6@gmail.com

Printed in Great Britain
by Amazon

59505694R00116